Twayne's English Authors Series

EDITOR OF THIS VOLUME

Kinley Roby

Northeastern University

Alex Comfort

TEAS 237

photo by James B. Beckett

Alex Comfort

ALEX COMFORT

By ARTHUR E. SALMON

University of Dubuque

TWAYNE PUBLISHERS

A DIVISION OF G. K. HALL & CO., BOSTON

Library of Congress Cataloging in Publication Data
Salmon, Arthur E.
  Alex Comfort.

  (Twayne's English authors series ; TEAS 237)
  Bibliography: p. 159-61
  Includes index.
  1. Comfort, Alexander, 1920-   —Criticism
and interpretation.
PR6005.0388Z88   828'.9'1209   77-19149
ISBN 0-8057-6708-8

PR
6005
.0388
Z88

For Judith and Norah

Contents

About the Author

Arthur Edward Salmon is an assistant professor at the University of Dubuque where he teaches a broad spectrum of courses, including interdisciplinary courses which he created and which carry credit in four different departments and cover five areas: English, Political Science, Psychology, and Philosophy and Religious Studies. He also teaches more traditional courses in writing, Modern Drama, and Modern British Literature. He has also taught modern British and American literature and English composition, both as a teaching assistant at the University of Wisconsin at Madison, Wisconsin, and as an Instructor at the Center-System campus of the University of Wisconsin at Wausau, Wisconsin.

Although some of Professor Salmon's poetry has been published, *Alex Comfort* is his first major publication. As an undergraduate, contemplating a career as a research biochemist, Professor Salmon became acquainted with Comfort's views on neo-Romanticism. His interest in Comfort's literary career developed out of his graduate work at the University of Wisconsin. His B.A. is from Oklahoma City University where he did course work in the natural sciences and in religious studies. His M.A. in English is from the University of Illinois. And his Ph.D. (1974) is from the University of Wisconsin where as a graduate student he majored in English and minored in Theater and Drama.

Preface

Now known to many Americans as an expert on human sexual behavior, Alex Comfort was once regarded as a major figure of the British neo-Romantic movement. This book provides an analysis of his art and thought and is focused on his treatment of death and power, two closely related themes in his works. My approach developed out of an interest in investigating the possible implications to Comfort's works of his assertion in *Art and Social Responsibility* (1946) that the modern "romantic" has "two enemies, Death, and the obedient who, by conformity to power and irresponsibility, ally themselves with Death. . ." (p. 18). In analyzing Comfort's treatment of power, I have compared his works with those of other libertarian writers, as well as explored the relationship between Comfort's art and his sociological studies and literary criticism. Comfort's incorporation of material from such works into his art is considered, as is the degree to which his sociological and aesthetic theories inform and provide a basis for his art.

Chapter one explores the libertarian implications of some of Comfort's prose works. In addition, it contains biographical information largely extracted from my August 7, 1974, recorded conversation with Comfort. Although he has written short stories and plays, as a literary artist Comfort has distributed his efforts primarily between his novels and his poetry. Chapter two treats Comfort's early novels—*The Almond Tree, No Such Liberty,* and *The Power House*—and the relationship between his fiction and his literary criticism (in particular, his *The Novel and Our Time,* 1948). Chapter three treats his later novels—*On This Side Nothing, A Giant's Strength,* and *Come Out to Play*—and Comfort's relationship to novelists such as Huxley, Camus, and Kafka. Chapter four is about Comfort's poetry, and the final chapter is about his artistic and intellectual significance.

A number of earlier critics, such as George Orwell and Anthony Thwaite, have been generally content to call attention to the unsoundness of the moral or political views and attitudes expressed by Comfort or his protagonists. On the other hand much earlier criticism has been written by persons who embrace his political conclusions. My own philosophical and political assumptions, which differ from those of Comfort, have been excluded as much as possible from my analysis of his works. An objective approach will hopefully prove useful to persons interested in Comfort's art. It may also prove helpful to critics interested in Comfort's literary career in order to understand more fully the nature and dimensions of British neo-Romanticism.

Comfort is a prolific and multidimensional writer. During the 1940s Kenneth Rexroth noted that he has "a universality about him in many ways reminiscent of Albert Schweitzer." My approach in treating his nonliterary works has been limited to exploring the implications of such works to his interest in the problems of death and power. One of Comfort's plays and his autobiographical *The Silver River* are discussed, but, similarly, for illustrative purposes.

Acknowledgments

Grateful acknowledgment is made for permission from the following: the author and Chapman and Hall, Ltd., for quotations from *The Almond Tree, No Such Liberty,* and *The Silver River;* the author and Routledge & Kegan Paul, Ltd., for quotations from *Ageing: The Biology of Senescence* and *Darwin and the Naked Lady;* the author and Eyre & Spottiswoode, Ltd., for quotations from *Haste to the Wedding* and *Come Out to Play;* the author and George Weidenfeld & Nicholson, Ltd., for quotations from *Nature and Human Nature;* the author and J. M. Dent & Sons, Ltd., for quotations from *The Novel and Our Time;* the author for quotations from his other published works.

The selections quoting George Orwell are from *My Country Right Or Left,* Volume 2 of *The Collected Essays, Journalism and Letters of George Orwell,* edited by Sonia Orwell and Ian Angus, copyright © 1968 by Sonia Brownell Orwell. Reprinted by permission of Harcourt Brace Jovanovich, Inc.

Chronology

1920   February 10, Alexander Comfort born, London: Parents, Daisy Elizabeth (Fenner) and Alexander Charles Comfort.

1932   Awarded foundation scholarship at Highgate School, where he is twice a Gold Medalist in Classics.

1936   Sails to South America as "captain's secretary" on a tramp steamer during his vacation.

1938   First book published: *The Silver River: Being the Diary of a Schoolboy in the South Atlantic, 1936*. Goes to Cambridge on the Robert Styring Scholarship in Classics, where he becomes Senior Scholar in Natural Sciences of Trinity College.

1940   Becomes Scholar of the London Hospital.

1941   Publication of *France and Other Poems*, his first volume of poetry, and *No Such Liberty*, his first novel.

1942   *Elegies* and *A Wreath for the Living*, volumes of poetry; *The Almond Tree*, a novel; and *Into Egypt: A Miracle Play*. Becomes coeditor with Robert Greacen of *Lyra: an Anthology of New Lyric* and coeditor with Peter Wells of *Poetry Folios*.

1943   *Cities of the Plain*, a play. Marries Ruth Muriel Harris.

1944   *The Power House*, a novel. Becomes coeditor with John Bayliss of *New Road: New Directions in European Art and Letters*. Earns from Cambridge degrees as Bachelor of Medicine and Bachelor of Surgery. Becomes Resident Medical Officer at Royal Waterloo Hospital, London.

1945   American publication of *The Power House* (by Viking Press). Publication of *The Song of Lazarus*, a volume of poetry. Earns an M.A. from Cambridge and a Diploma in Child Health from the University of London. Becomes Lecturer in Physiology at London Hospital Medical College.

1946   *Art and Social Responsibility*, a philosophical and sociological explanation of the New Romanticism. Translates with Ross MacDougall Ramuz's *Présence de la Mort* into English.

1947   *Letters from an Outpost*, a collection of short stories, and *The Signal to Engage*, a volume of poetry.

1948   *The Novel and Our Time, Barbarism and Sexual Freedom,* and
        First-Year Physiological Technique.

1949   *On This Side Nothing,* a novel. Receives a Ph.D. in
        Biochemistry from the University of London for research into
        the nature of molluscan shell pigments.

1950   *Authority and Delinquency in the Modern State,* an attempt to
        apply "the method of criminology to the 'criminals in office,'"
        and *The Pattern of the Future,* the text of broadcast talks
        delivered on the BBC in 1949 (the BBC amends for Comfort's
        having been blacklisted in wartime for pacifism).

1951   *And All But He Departed,* a volume of poetry. Becomes
        Honorary Research Associate, Department of Zoology, Uni-
        versity College, London.

1952   *A Giant's Strength,* a novel. Becomes Nuffield Research
        Fellow in Biology of Senescence, University College, Lon-
        don.

1956   *The Biology of Senescence.*

1958   Receives the Ciba Foundation Prize for research on gerontol-
        ogy.

1961   *Come Out to Play,* a novel, and *The Process of Ageing.*

1962   *Haste to the Wedding,* a volume of poetry, and *Darwin and the
        Naked Lady,* essays on biology and art. Receives the Bore-
        stone Poetry Award. Jailed with Bertrand Russell for organiz-
        ing an antinuclear sitdown in London's Trafalgar Square.

1963   *Sex in Society.* Conferred Doctor of Science (Gerontology) by
        the University of London.

1965   Publication in English of *The Koka Shastra,* translated and
        with an introduction by Comfort.

1966   *Nature and Human Nature,* a biological and social study which
        "gives us with admirable succinctness," according to Anthony
        Burgess, "the human situation as it stands at present and how
        it came about." Becomes Director of the Medical Research
        Group on the Biology of Ageing at University College, Lon-
        don.

1967   *The Anxiety Makers,* an analysis of the historical causes of
        anxiety concerning sexual behavior. Serves as President of the
        British Society for Research on Ageing.

1972   *The Joy of Sex,* a "Cordon Bleu Guide to Lovemaking."

1973   Marries Jane Tristram Henderson, a sociologist at the London
        School of Economics whom he had known as a fellow student
        at Cambridge.

Chronology

1974 Emigrates to Santa Barbara, California, to become a Senior Fellow at the Center for the Study of Democratic Institutions at Santa Barbara, California. Publication of *More Joy.*

1975 Republication of *Sex in Society* and *Come Out to Play.* After the collapse of the Center, joins the Institute for Higher Studies for research and education in the areas of "biology, social and constitutional systems, systems analysis, and computer modeling and simulation for the investigation of historical, linguistic and futurological problems."

1976 *A Good Age,* a self-defense manual for older people.

1978 Anticipated publication of another volume of poetry, a book on the biology of religion *(I and That),* and several science-fiction works: *A Fearful Symmetry, A Grain of Sand,* and *Beyond the Night of Beulah.*

CHAPTER 1

Against Death and Power

IN *The Freedom of Poetry* (1947) Derek Stanford reiterates Charles
Hamblett's description of Alexander Comfort as "the Voltaire of
neo-Romanticism."[1] Although Stanford is thinking primarily of his
"public-minded thinking," the comparison suggests something of the
range of Comfort's literary endeavors. He has published six novels, a
short-story collection, seven volumes of poetry, two plays, and, as
early as 1938, an autobiographical travelogue of considerable merit
entitled *The Silver River*. He has translated *The Koka Shastra* (an
Indian manual of sexual techniques, analogous to *The Kama Sutra*),
cotranslated Charles-Ferdinand Ramuz's *Présence de la Mort*, and
coedited three periodical literary anthologies, *Lyra*, *Poetry Folios*,
and *New Road*. Moreover, he is one of the few contemporary writers
to have combined a successful after-hours literary career with a
continuous and extremely successful career having nothing to do with
literature: Comfort is generally recognized as the foremost gerontologist of the twentieth century. He has also shown surprising
competence in other areas, having published a textbook on physiological technique, a number of sociological studies, and, more recently,
manuals on sexual behavior entitled *The Joy of Sex* and *More Joy*.
Comfort has, as well, published hundreds of articles, editorials,
reviews, and pamphlets pertaining to the various areas described
above.

His literary significance is indicated by G. S. Fraser, who notes
that "during the Second World War, he was regarded as the leading
figure in a broad movement" sometimes called the New Romanticism, or neo-Romanticism.[2] (The Apocalyptic writers, Henry Treece,
G. S. Fraser, J. F. Hendry, Vernon Watkins, Nicholas Moore, and
others, "were among the very first writers," T. H. Helmstadter has
observed, "of what became a wide literary trend . . . described as a
New Romanticism."[3]) Comfort is also the most important contem-

17

porary artist representing anarchist ideas and policies. His political views and his views on sexual behavior anticipate the political radicalism and new sexual morality of the late 1960s and 1970s. Nicolas Walter properly sees Comfort's *Sexual Behavior in Society* (1950) as "an early call for what came to be known as the 'new morality' or the 'permissive society.'. . . ."[4]

I *Biographical Perspectives*

He was born on February 10, 1920. Comfort's mother, a "very brilliant academic," devoted much time to his personal education. His father was "a mentor also at the university" as well as a "municipal servant in London." There is not "very much relationship" between his early libertarian views and the views of his parents. "I think I acquired some of the attributes of both of them, as one does of parents, but I don't think they had any special bearing on the views I expressed," Comfort observes. Politically, his father was "not exactly a formal socialist, but had one very close friend who was an influence in the old days of the Labor Party." On sexual morality his parent's ideas "were very much middle of the road."[5]

He went to Highgate School and, later, to Cambridge " 'on scholarships, not on privilege.' "[6] "Highgate was the school Poet Laureate John Betjeman attended" as well as the "school where T. S. Eliot," years earlier, was "employed as a master," Hugh Kenner notes in an article on Comfort written for the *New York Times*.[7] Comfort attributes his interest in Classics, "and much other fructive awakening,"[8] to his schoolmasters at Highgate. Twice a Gold Medalist in Classics at Highgate, in 1938 he went to Cambridge on the Robert Styring Scholarship in Classics where he became Senior Scholar in Natural Sciences of Trinity College and was awarded a First Class in Part I of the Natural Science Tripos in 1940. Partly as the result of his Classical education, his writings tend to have, as he says, a "Classical apparatus which isn't very obvious at first sight."[9]

His scientific interests began "early." Comfort "started with chemistry," engaging in chemistry experiments until he was injured in "a homemade firework explosion" in 1934. His attention then shifted to natural history generally and to mollusks in particular. (Later, at the University of London, Comfort did his doctoral dissertation "on the biochemistry of molluscan shell pigments.") Such scientific interests are evident in Comfort's autobiographical *The Silver River* (subtitled "The Diary of a Schoolboy in the South Atlantic, 1936" and published in 1938) in which he describes his

travels "under the guise of an amateur naturalist" (p. 8). The work is of
primary significance as the only written record of his youthful mind.
   According to Harold Drasdo *The Silver River*

is a record of ten weeks at sea during the summer of 1936. Comfort sailed with
his father on a Dutch tramp to Buenos Aires, calling at Madeira; they
returned on a Greek boat *via* Dakar. His narrative consists of impressions of
place and seascape, of notes on life and manners, of botanical and zoological
observations. The young author writes already with an impressive assurance.
He is an idealist with an engaging sense of humour; more remarkably, he is a
precise observer and very well-informed student of natural history. There is a
feeling of receptiveness, of an insatiable curiosity, in his book and yet, from
this admirable beginning, no one could have deduced much about the novels
which were to follow.[10]

   Deducing much from *The Silver River* about the novels which were
to follow, Robert Callahan finds its author to be "no transcenden-
talist." Rather, *The Silver River* reveals "a general sociological stoi-
cism or pessimism which is extended and elaborated in Comfort's
later writings. . . ."[11] Comfort was a "liberal Christian"[12] at the time
he wrote the work, however. In it he suggests, moreover, that it is the
orderliness and beauty of nature which provide the guarantee—
missing in his later works—that human life is meaningful and values
are absolute. In chapter four, for example, young Comfort at sea
describes a tropical Atlantic sunset, and his description suggests the
nineteenth-century Romantic myth that the child has insights which
are lost with the fall into adult consciousness. This tropical sunset
"carries the essence of all human art in itself," and gives

a momentary glimpse of something which I knew once quite well, but have
forgotten. I recapture that sunset with its fugitive recollection in music now
and then: it is hidden in the "Tragic Overture" of Brahms, and it flashes for a
second, now and again, in Mendelssohn and Wagner. There was a full
orchestra in the clouds that night, and I have heard the symphony which it
played, the bold theme given out on brass and drums and echoed round the
horizon by all the instruments, but I cannot remember it. I suppose it was the
music of the spheres. (pp. 43–44)

   Arguing for the development in self-awareness of the narrator on a
pattern somewhat analogous to that of the *bildungsroman*, Callahan
treats Comfort's description of the symphony in the sky as an example
of "pictoral intensity . . . effected through forced, self-conscious
lyricism. . . ." He goes on to conclude:

As I read *The Silver River*, Comfort illuminates an awakening of his own social emotions by moving from such breath-taking but artificial heightening of observation toward the imagery of comparatively objective pictorialism, as, for example, in the images selected to re-create the atmosphere of the evening on which the Argosy arrived at Goree Bay, Dakar. . . .[13]

Arrival at port, however, signals for Comfort an end of such visionary experiences elicited, as in Wordsworth, by relatively uncivilized, natural settings. Comparatively objective pictorialism always accompanies descriptions of civilization, as, for example, in the opening paragraph treating the platform activity at Hook of Holland (pp. 9–10), and in the narrator's concluding remarks at the end of his journey: "To-morrow, Liverpool. The dimensions of time and space will return" (p. 160). Moreover, the preface establishes the antithesis to be maintained throughout the work. After the experience of escape into the "real world" beyond the precincts of civilization, "the sordidness of port comes as a shock" (p. 7). This visionary experience is not diminished by Comfort's experiences of the injustices of the capitalistic, urbanized, and industrialized society of Buenos Aires with its horrifying slums. It is made more relevant and necessary as a moral and spiritual antidote or corrective to the cynicism, despair and moral myopia which civilization fosters.

After leaving Buenos Aires, Comfort travels to La Plata, the original seat of government. It is happily free from the noise and the "hot anxiety" of Buenos Aires, and is a "town which has stopped, run down." Comfort hopes that "nobody tries to wind it up—I should like to stay there" (p. 107). To an extent such observations reflect Comfort's role as a curious traveler whose narrations display his historical interests and love of pictorial detail. But they also point to a shoreside alternative available to those who are disenchanted with the stifling, violent environment provided by the megalopolis.

In its view of the psychopathological atmosphere of the megalopolis, as stated in the preface and illustrated in Comfort's description of Buenos Aires, *The Silver River* does significantly anticipate his later works. The emissaries of unscrupulous foriegn industrialists hold the reins of power in Buenos Aires. The system of capitalism has contributed towards the development of "two populations," the fragmentation of society into the "industrialists and the hereditarily wealthy" opposed to the "factory operatives." It has also created one of the "vilest slums" that the narrator has ever seen (pp. 89–91). Comfort prophesies that a revolution, which will end not only "capitalism in the Argentine," but also "the interference of British capital in the South Atlantic once and for all," is inevitable (p. 91). Whether the revolution will be "from the right," as in Brazil, or from the left, he is not prepared to guess. But it appears likely that the "nation of the Barracas" (i.e., the proletariat, the destitute of the slums), who "are beginning to realize their strength and to call for the public ownership of railroads and industry" (p. 91), will provide the revolution with an essentially socialist orientation.

In the philosophical determinism of Marx revolutions are inevitably generated by the economic exploitation of the proletariat. In *The Silver River* Comfort, who finds in nature a source of meaning and moral values, indicates that the certainty of change is primarily guaranteed by the fundamentally moral, and consequently rational, character of the universe in which such changes occur:

One thing is certain. Such abject poverty and such wasteful and rampant vice have never been permitted throughout history to continue without bringing their due reward to the authors of the condition. That reward is coming in Buenos Aires to a corrupt officialdom and a cynical and inhuman party of speculators. It will come with exceptional violence. I have seen it on the way. (p. 92)

After *The Silver River* Comfort wrote on "A New Variety of *Mya Arenaria*" (published in the *Journal of Conchology,* September 22, 1938). But then, in the early 1940s as an undergraduate at Cambridge, he seemed to burst into print. In addition to writing novels, poetry, plays, and becoming editor of *Lyra* and *Poetry Folios,* Comfort began writing articles on poetry, the novel, film, pacifism, et cetera, for *Horizon, The Spectator, Poetry Quarterly, Life and Letters Today, Partisan Review,* and other periodicals. In 1943 for *Partisan Review* Comfort wrote that the "youngest poets" are facing an attack, partly from the Georgians, "whose line is briefly a demand that the young poets should become the literary propagandists of the war, devote themselves to the study of Brooks, and write choric odes to the Air Force. . . ."[14] Refusing to be a propagandist, Comfort publicly denounced the war. Because he finally headed the agitation against indiscriminate bombing, he was officially blacklisted by the BBC.

As a conscientious objector Comfort pursued his medical studies at Cambridge. In 1943 he was for a few months a student in Dublin because there were few "women and children in London, owing to the evacuation," to treat in family-practice courses. The Irish background stayed with him. A number of his poems "could be Irish." The allusions and "scenic background" are occasionally Irish. Some contain "references to places like Rush in Ireland," and a number of the scenes depicted "were also the background of Yeats's poetry in county Sligo." He also remembers visiting Arthur Koestler during the early 1940s, "finding him stripped to the waist with a huge pile of psychoanalytic textbooks which he was engaged in incorporating into a novel." (It was probably Koestler's *Arrival and Departure*, published in 1943.) Comfort acknowledges that his description in *The Power House* (1944) of a textile worker "climbing the chimney" of a French factory represents a similar incorporation of Freudian material.[15]

From the first Comfort's literary works had a strong European emphasis. His early education, probably his mother's tutoring in particular, is of some significance in this respect. He "read French from an early age" and is "nearly as familiar with French literature as with English. So the European influence is probably French." But he also started writing novels "during the war when Europe was where it was at, and when it was becoming very important to assert the unity of Britain with the Europe we were cut off from by the war." Moreover, he experienced during the war feelings of "terrible alienation" from British society because he "wanted no part of any of the things the government at the time was doing." But he didn't "entirely identify with Europe either." It was "more identifying with the people in all countries who were opposed to both sides in the war and to what was going on." "You see," Comfort explains, "we damn nearly in Britain—it isn't widely realized—got into the war on Hitler's side because we were about to intervene in Finland against the Russians on the same side as the Germans. Then, very shortly afterwards, the same government was declaring war on Germany." From an "ideological point of view there was nothing to be said for Churchill and his 'unconditional surrender.' " Comfort felt he had "more in common with some of the people in the French resistance, or even some of the people who were being persecuted both by the Germans and the French resistance because they wouldn't take sides with either of them"[16]

A number of his prose writings, poems, and novels echo the sense of alienation and expatriation evident in his reflections above. Breitz in *No Such Liberty* (1941) is the first of Comfort's protagonists to recognize the personal nightmare of what Breitz refers to as "exile and impotence" (p. 54). Pacifist anarchists generally during the 1940s experienced a profound sense of exile and expatriation. But the war, producing European refugees, universalized the anarchist experience: hence, Comfort's creation of Breitz in *No Such Liberty*, Shmul in *On This Side Nothing* (1949), and Hedler in *A Giant's Strength* (1952)—all literally men without countries. George Woodcock in his anarchist "Poem from London, 1941" expresses sentiments which could appropriately stand as the epigraph to much of Comfort's art: "kissed onward by the pistol, we are all exile, / Expatriate, wandering in the illusive streets / Of faked identity."

According to Kenner, during the 1950s and 1960s BBC listeners knew Comfort as an anarcho-pacifist philosopher, "officialdom occasionally yanking the mike from in front of him. In the days when Eden and Nasser were eyeball to eyeball, the BBC wouldn't let Comfort cry 'Stop Suez!' but he cried it anyway, breaking into the evening newscasts from a mobile transmitter Scotland Yard never tracked down."[17] Also during this period Comfort and Bertrand Russell became friends and fellow members of the famous Committee of One Hundred. Many of his libertarian ideas, especially those on sex, parallel Russell's. But Comfort knew Russell when he had "already intellectually developed," and, consequently, his agreement with Russell's views "has really been post hoc."[18] In 1962 both were jailed for organizing an antinuclear sitdown in London's Trafalgar Square.

The publication of *The Biology of Senescence* in 1956 established Comfort's reputation as a gerontologist. It became a "text for innumerable students," Kenner observes, "in part because it is so much better written than any other overview on the shelves. . . ."[19] In 1958 Comfort received the Ciba Foundation Prize for research on gerontology. Gerontological references appear in two of his novels published after 1948 (*On This Side Nothing* and *A Giant's Strength*). Both works reflect his growing interest in the possibility of combating death and the ageing process through scientific research. In contrast, a sense of the inescapability of death, or the triumph of death, characterizes his earlier literary works.

II *Struggling Against Death*

Commenting on the significance of Classical and Romantic tendencies in literature, Comfort in *Art and Social Responsibility* (1946) writes, "It is as if the awareness of death, the factor which, at root, determines the degree to which we feel masters of our circumstances, ebbed and flowed, alternately emphasised and obscured as a factor in interpretative art" (p. 14). If consciousness of death has ebbed and flowed, the modern period is for Comfort one in which it has overflowed. His translation (with Allan Ross MacDougall) of Charles-Ferdinand Ramuz's *Présence de lat Mort* (1925) into English with an English title of *The Triumph of Death* (1946) was undoubtedly motivated in part by the fact that Ramuz's novel provides an arresting allegorical presentation of a widescale preoccupation with death in the modern period. In Ramuz's highly poetic novel an approaching cosmic catastrophe focuses the mind of everyone upon death:

> Then the great, inaudible words came. The great message was sent from one continent to another, across the water. . . .
> Today like all other days, and as if it would always be just so: only that the big invisible words have been spoken, giving the result of long calculation and careful research: the earth is falling towards the sun.
> Something has happened to the law of gravity. The earth is rapidly falling towards the sun, rushing to rejoin it.
> So all life will come to an end. The temperature will go up and everything will rapidly die.[20]

The English title given to Ramuz's novel recalls Francesco Traini's *The Triumph of Death* as well as Gabriele D'Annunzio's story of love and suicide, *Il Trionfo del Morte*. But the choice of the title was probably influenced primarily by Pieter Brueghel's *The Triumph of Death* to which Comfort alludes in *The Power House*, and which he praises in *Art and Social Responsibility* for its humane treatment of man's victimization by Death.

With respect to anxiety or fear concerning death, his position is similar to that expressed in existentialist literature as well as in much modern literature generally. For Comfort the human condition is defined largely on the basis of an awareness of death which human beings do not share with other primates, and such an awareness has serious moral implications. Either the individual confronts courageously and realistically the tragic fact of personal mortality, or he seeks to escape from an awareness of mortality by submerging his personality in the corporate existence of some group, organization, or institution based on authority or power. In *Art and Social Responsibility* he argues that the "negation of individual personality," and its accompanying sense of mortality, takes the "form of a growing belief in the conception of an immortal, invisible and only wise society. . . . Society is not only a form of abrogating moral responsibility, it is a womb into which one can crawl back and become immortal because unborn" (pp. 19–20). Such a line of reasoning anticipates Camus's argument in *The Rebel* that men attempt to escape from the realization of mortality by submerging themselves in the immortality of the human species,[21] and Clamence's observation in *The Fall* that "Death is solitary, whereas slavery is collective."[22]

Comfort's views are anticipated (if not influenced) by a description in Ramuz's *The Triumph of Death* of a group of men escaping from the knowledge of death. Realizing that the earth is falling towards the sun, some laborers who have been laying pipes forsake their work, become riotously intoxicated, and experience the forgetfulness of losing their individual identities: "being many yet but one—that was grand—being many, yet but a single person" (p. 72). Their story, chapter fifteen of Ramuz's novel, is, we are told, "merely a picture of what happens elsewhere," a picture "in miniature" (p. 65). The concomitant notion that an awareness of death has the positive function of awakening the individual to the seriousness and uniqueness of human existence (pp. 18, 20, 28) bears some similarity to Comfort's belief that responsible, authentic existence involves accepting the fact of personal mortality. But Comfort, rather like Sartre, does not believe that death can be made a meaningful part of life. He also does not believe that an awareness of the uniqueness and seriousness of human existence is fundamentally dependent upon an awareness of its precariousness or brevity.

The Romantic's insecurity in the face of death as defined by Comfort is distinguishable from the notion in existentialism that dread is a response to the confrontation with nothingness. Nothingness or nonbeing has no discernible status in Comfort's thought as it does in existentialist thought which springs from Heidegger (*Sein und Zeit*, 1927). For Comfort nothingness is the absence of being— the conventional common sense as well as scientific assumption— rather than a metaphysical reality. In his works, and particularly in the elegies, death is metaphorically included in being, a notion reminiscent of the Heideggerian assumption that nonbeing is at the core of being. The elegies recount "how death in living labours in our bones." However, death is being defined as a physical process, similar to Dylan Thomas's definition of death as "a process in the weather of the heart" turning "damp to dry," and not as a metaphysical reality at the center of being.

For Comfort, as for Thomas, the process of death is the process of ageing (Thomas's "Worm beneath my nail/Wearing the quick away"), involving the gradual death of the physical organism. The

emotional reaction which accompanies an awareness of death (Comfort speaks of the realization of "the emotional fact of death"[23]) is
partly a reaction to such a gradual disintegration of the body. In
Ageing: The Biology of Senescence (1964) Comfort notes that the
"uniformity of this process is one of the earliest unpleasant discoveries which every individual has to make, and although we have
many psychological expedients to blunt its impact, the fact of this
effective fixity of life-span, and of the decline in activity and health
which often determines it, is always in the background of the human
mind" (p. 1).

His gerontological career is a logical outgrowth of the intermixture
in his personality of his medical interests and his belief that death is
one of humanity's primary enemies. On the other hand his medical
background plays a part in forming his particular emphasis upon the
struggle against death as one of man's major concerns. Ageing,
defined in Comfort's *The Process of Ageing* (1961) as the "Last
Enemy," is for Comfort a remedial process, at least in theory. His
optimism concerning the possibility of slowing down or reversing the
ageing process developed gradually, and parallels, approximately,
the development of the science of gerontology, which he sees as
beginning about 1950. Although believing in *The Process of Ageing*
that it is theoretically possible to modify the ageing process, now
Comfort reportedly believes (according to statements made by him in
a 1970 interview in *Time* magazine) that

because of advances in genetics and molecular biology . . . some method to
reduce the rate of ageing and to extend vigorous life by at least 15 years will be
discovered within the next two decades. This extension would be in addition
to the roughly five-to-seven year increase in average life expectancy that will
take place when medicine conquers cancer and vascular diseases.[24]

Since it is now rather widely known that the life-span of mice has
been increased by the use of chemical additives in their diets, and, in
the 1930s, through underfeeding,[25] Comfort's optimism concerning
the possibility of prolonging the useful human life-span cannot be
considered to be greatly exaggerated. It also is not a defense
mechanism against confronting the fact of death. On the other hand,
hostility to the attempt by scientists to impede or reverse the ageing
process, Comfort observes in *The Process of Ageing*, may represent a
"denial of a very deeply felt anxiety" (p. 17).

If we seek a further explanation of Comfort's optimistic efforts and attitudes along these lines, his libertarian orientation may be of some significance. The process of ageing is retarded in William Morris's quasi-anarchist *News from Nowhere*. William Godwin in *St. Leon* is preoccupied with a hero who has discovered the alchemist's key to eternal youth (but with some disastrous consequences because St. Leon has made his own continued existence a merely selfish consideration). In *Enquiry Concerning Political Justice* Godwin speaks hopefully of the possibility of retarding the ageing process. (Contrast the pessimism concerning prolonging life which characterizes Swift's treatment of the Struldbrugs, Tennyson's use of the Tithonus myth, and Eliot's use of the myth of Sibyls.) An anarchist rebellion against power or coercive control may tend to affirm the value of life against the tyranny of the repressive and destructive processes of nature as well.

III   *"To defy Power, which seems omnipotent"—Shelley*

The ideas of other libertarian writers do not necessarily have a cause-and-effect bearing on any particular idea Comfort expresses: "I arrived in most cases at my own opinions and then, having read other people, found that what they . . . said was in line with these," he observes. The ideas of other libertarian writers, however, do provide connections and indicate a historical perspective for Comfort's art and thought. His early views, for example, in some respects parallel those of Herbert Read, the major intellectual influence upon the Apocalyptic writers. Comfort dedicated *Art and Social Responsibility* to Read, "liked him immensely," and "spent afternoons with him on occasion." According to Comfort, "Read's great discovery was the way in which the integration of art into education could make for a much more libertarian and a much broader approach to nonartistic matters—let's say art as a form of liberation. This was the thing he preached throughout."[26]

In asserting in *Art and Social Responsibility* that it is fundamentally the awareness of death which distinguishes Romanticism from Classicism, Comfort significantly departs from Read. But their views of history are in other respects similar. According to Comfort in *Art and Social Responsibility*, the history of power, rather than a progression, is an "oscillation about a fixed point, a series of self-limiting ecological changes, an ebb and flow between certain fixed limits . . ." (p. 16). Such a view of institutionalized power is reflected in his view of literary history:

These terms, classic and romantic, stand for more than differences of style. The classic sees man as master, the romantic sees him as victim of his environment. That seems to me to be the real difference. I regard the periods of English literature as an alternation between these two concepts. (p. 14)

His belief that Romanticism and Classicism represent alternating tendencies and that both should be defined in essentially ideological, rather than stylistic, terms is anticipated by Herbert Read in *Reason and Romanticism*, as well as by T. E. Hulme. Read links Romanticism and Classicism to "an opposition between" two "sets of cultural values" which have "always existed" and which correspond "to deep-rooted psychological orientations which from time to time alternate in their dominance."[27] Classical periods have an "extroverted public," Comfort concludes in *Art and Social Responsibility* (p. 14), and Read notes in *Reason and Romanticism* the "extroverted and introverted types which are analogues to cultural types."[28] Comfort also follows Read in identifying Classicism with oppressive political power and the struggle against such power with Romanticism. Read remarks in *Reason and Romanticism* that Classicism

represents for us now, and has always represented, the forces of oppression. Classicism is the intellectual counterpart of political tyranny. It was so in the ancient world and in the medieval empires; it was renewed to express the dictatorships of the Renaissance and has ever since been the official creed of capitalism. Wherever the blood of martyrs stains the ground, there you will find a doric column or perhaps a statue of Minerva.[29]

In opposition to the popular notion of historical progress, either by perfecting existing institutions or by acquiring new institutions through revolution, Comfort believes in the transformation of society largely through the transformation of the individual. Similarly, Henry Treece, influenced by the anarchist Romanticism of Read, writes in *How I See Apocalypse* that what he is primarily asking for is "A CHANGE OF HEART."[30] An emphasis on social change through personal redemption is ubiquitous in anarchist thought and is usually linked with utopian implications. The transformation of society envisioned by Shelley in *Prometheus Unbound* begins at the level of the moral transformation or regeneration of Prometheus. Godwin's *Imogen* is similarly an allegory of the transformation of society through the development of individual benevolence and reason. The curse pronounced upon Godwin's Roderick, who represents the forces of tyranny and oppression, points towards the realization that society cannot be transformed by violent revolution. It may be transformed by individuals who, in imitation of the pattern set by Imogen, have been themselves transformed. Roderick is cursed with the knowledge that when a "Simple Maid" shall "resist all His Personal Attractions and all His Power: Then Shall his Power be at an End."[31]

What is distinctive in Comfort's anarchism is the absence of any optimistic belief that individual redemption will necessarily result in the ultimate redemption of society generally. Traditionally anarchists have posited anarchist societies at both ends of the historical spectrum. In this sense the traditional anarchist view of history resembles the tripartite view of history in Christianity: Eden, expulsion into a period of persecution by and conflict against the demonic powers-that-be, and, ultimately, Paradise regained. Exploiting the popular notion of the Golden Age, Godwin in *Imogen* represents the utopian period before the development of government, laws, and rulers, and intimates a future period in which the world of Imogen will be recaptured, in which government and tyrannical power will have ceased to exist. Comfort speculates on the origins of government in *Authority and Delinquency* (1950), but stresses that the notion of a primitive anarchist utopia is another idealistic oversimplification of the historical process, a myth embodying human aspirations: "If there is or was a Golden Age, its existence is in the human mind rather than in concrete societies" (p. 105). A future anarchist society is also a mythical possibility in Comfort's works in the sense that there is no foreseeable, final end to power-orientation within society.

The absence in Comfort's works of statements on the character of a future anarchist society is not, consequently, simply a matter of his acceptance of the conventional anarchist posture of reticence. Other anarchists, such as Read, do not theorize in depth on the nature of a noncoercive society. They argue that it is imprudent to plan rational blueprints that will inevitably be negated by unpredictable future needs and contingencies. But rather than viewing mankind as moving towards an ambiguous anarchist utopia, Comfort settles his attention, in both his sociological and literary works, on the unending conflict between the responsible individual and irresponsible society. He is very close to the spirit of Camus's *The Rebel* when he argues in *Art and Social Responsibility* that "revolution is not a single act, it is an unending process based upon individual disobedience" (p. 29), and in *The Pattern of the Future* (1950) that

we have got to be willing to live, to disobey. . . . Remember that *this*
revolution, the revolution towards sociality, has no further side, when we can
all relax. . . . (p. 52)

His attitude towards revolution as an unending process (what Camus
refers to as rebellion as opposed to revolution) anticipates, and
probably influences, an important change in British anarchism during the late 1950s. In an essay on the history of contemporary British
anarchism, David Stafford notes that while "the New Left has been
moving closer to the anarchists, the anarchists have been moving
away from their traditional posture; and if one of the characteristics of
the New Left in the 1960s is what has been described as 'The
Balkanization of Utopia,' then one of the characteristics of the anarchists has been its abolition."[32]

IV *Decentralizing*

Although coercive government cannot in the foreseeable future be
eliminated, it can be decentralized, Comfort believes. His antipathy
towards centralization (or the megalopolis) is already at work in *The
Silver River* and continues in his later writings. Arguing for a modification of social attitudes and structures which would foster sexual
well-being, Comfort in *Sex in Society* (1963) writes of the desirability
of consciously planned decentralized communities which would incorporate the "entire range of potentialities which exist in technology
. . ." (p. 151). Decentralizing society is also Comfort's concern in
Cities of the Plain, a play, published in 1943 but written in 1940. Its
mythological structure is reflected in Comfort's more important
literary works, discussed in subsequent chapters.

In *The Freedom of Poetry* Derek Stanford notes that *Cities of the
Plain* is

laid in a kind of proletarian Ruritania; and instead of shakos, battle-scenes,
and waltzes we have miners' dinner-pails, malnutrition, and strikes. A
crooked business syndicate, with municipal and ecclesiastic assistance, has
enslaved the population. The climax of their unscrupulousness is a plan to
send the miners down to extract a precious ore which burns and rots their
bones. Led By Dr. Manson, the miners rebel, while the representatives of
other employments—the chemists and the busmen—join their ranks.[33]

Stanford believes that although Comfort "takes a political term to
qualify the title of this play," he "obviously does not intend to act the
town-crier for any political party. . . ."[34] The title, however, alludes

to the biblical story of Sodom and Gomorrah: "God destroyed the cities of the plain . . ." (Genesis 19:29). Like ancient Sodom and Gomorrah, the city of Comfort's play is materialistic and corrupt and destined to receive a fiery judgment rained down from heaven. The mountain which is being mined explodes like Vesuvius.

The chronological as well as thematic movement of *Cities of the Plain* is from decentralization to greater and greater degrees of centralization, from a minimum of power (governmental, economic, and technological power) to a maximum of power until, to borrow an analogy from physics, a kind of critical mass is reached. The explosion of the mountain, the play's dominant symbol of power, suggests that the modern process of social and industrial centralization contains within itself the principle of its own destruction. The accompanying insurrection of the miners is possibly meant to suggest the anarcho-syndicalist myth of the revolutionary general strike. For the syndicalists the general strike would have the effect of destroying the rule of governmment itself, but it would not involve a seizure of governmental power. In any case the final eruption of the mountain means the destruction of centralized power, rather than its transference to a new governing elite. Such power is destroyed by being decentralized and redistributed, as is the mountain's strength in its fiery flow of lava. The symbolic conclusion intimates such meanings:

> The feet of the miners passing
> have swept as fire on the plain.
> The future sings to the present,
> the dead are alive again. . . .
> Here is the blow and the token
> Our strength is upon us again.

In 1974 Comfort more directly expressed his continuing conviction that government must be "decentralized" as much as possible. "I think that the political movements that are important in the present-day society," Comfort remarked, "are the protest movements, the movements for neighborhood action, neighborhood control, and in fact all of the ways in which the government at the center does get its head held under water by the periphery."

V *Towards a Libertarian Sexology*

Comfort's works treat the unending conflict between individual responsibility and conformist thinking. His early scientific interests and training, however, assist in making it a conflict between the scientific method and prescientific modes of thinking and feeling. He sees himself as engaged in the task of directing society's attention to the "possibility of superseding politics by the scientific method. . ." (*Sex in Society*, p. 152). Such an attitude is present in his attempts to supplant prescientific attitudes towards sexual behavior and its control by contemporary biological and sociological insights.

The conventional assumption is that social control must be based on punishment and the fear of punishment. What is punishable behavior is defined in reference to religious and secular authority. Sexual aberrations have first been defined as "sinful." As Comfort reminds his readers in his criticism of the medical profession, *The Anxiety Makers* (1967), such aberrations have more recently been defined as "abnormal" and, hence, undesirable.

In *Nature and Human Nature* (1969) Comfort makes normative judgments about human nature. But one such judgment, apparently based on the research of writers such as Roger Williams on individual variability, is that human physiology and disposition are subject to wide inbuilt variations (see chapter four). Conventional morality and legality, Comfort's works imply, fail to take such variations into consideration. Furthermore, he avoids the term "abnormal," particularly in *The Joy of Sex* (1972) and *More Joy* (1974), presumably because it is often the instrument of repressive society, a form of punishment through social disapproval. (The same, of course, applies to earlier definitions of sexual aberrations as "sinful.")

His objections to punishment generally, including the more specialized use in psychology of aversive therapy, intersect those of B. F. Skinner in *Science and Human Behavior*. Punishment often merely leads to avoidance behavior, Skinner argues. Comfort similarly notes in *More Joy* that society "has for centuries tried to turn off unpopular forms of behavior by aversion (punishment) without much success, because they usually managed to reinforce not being found out" (p. 184). Positive reinforcement of desirable behavior, in other words, is far preferable.

The treatment of homosexuality through aversion—*Clockwork Orange* fashion—provides an example. The homosexual, Comfort argues, "doesn't need to lose what is a normal human reaction. What he needs to acquire is a skill he hasn't acquired, that of relating to women, so that what you need to do is to reinforce his heterosexual experience, if that's what he wants."[35] The emphasis in Comfort's works is on "if that's what he wants," upon nondirective assistance rather that upon imposing criteria of morality or normalcy. Encouraging heterosexual or bisexual experience through behaviorist means—by positive reinforcements (or rewards)—fosters human dignity and freedom rather than goes "beyond" them, in Skinnerian terms. Positive reinforcement—giving the homosexual heterosexual experiences—involves creating a situation in which

he has reasonable choice, then, which of the two forms of behavior, or both, he feels it is appropriate for him to display, both in terms of his own needs and in terms of the social consequences of displaying them. You've actually, then, increased his freedom, because in the past his freedom was limited by the fact that there was one form of behavior which he was finding it difficult to display.[36]

Such a view of human freedom, however, is not necessarily in conflict with a deterministic view of human nature. Bertrand Russell similarly defines freedom in terms of human options rather than from the perspective of metaphysical speculation about ultimately undetermined human behavior.

Punishment, Comfort believes, "is merely psychopathic. It has nothing whatever to do with purpose. It's mainly to relieve the feelings of the punisher."[37] Legal, institutionalized punishment is an example. "There may be a few people in society who are so deranged or so dangerous to their fellows that they need to be excluded from society. But most of the people imprisoned don't need to be imprisoned at all for any rational purpose. It's part of an archaic ritual which does no good to anybody."[38] Aversive experiences generally can obviously not be completely avoided: for example, the environment, Skinner reminds his readers, often conditions aversively. But both Comfort and Skinner would agree that more efficient modes of altering behavior are available. Comfort, however, is patently not interested in moving from the repressive techniques of social control of *1984* to the generally nonaversive techniques of *Brave New World,* even a brave new world which has incorporated Skinnerian operant conditioning.

In opposition to such centrally organized and mechanistic programs, Comfort advocates biological and sociological controls. A mode of influencing social behavior is already to be found in the role that mores play in controlling behavior, even in the absence of a legal apparatus. In *Sex in Society* Comfort writes that the entire emphasis of the asocial society, in its attempts to control individual conduct and the manifestations of individual aggression, is still institutional. Both governments and revolutionary movements tend to look upon institutions as a means of salvation, to be upheld or altered. But older patterns of law rested ultimately on the traditional standards (*mores*) of the group, and from the observation of a society like our own, in which institutions exist increasingly in isolation, we can say with certainty that the part such institutions play in determining conduct is extremely limited. This is particularly obvious in sexual behavior, where the *mores* of individual strata of society bear little relationship to laws and are almost uninfluenced by them. (p. 51)

Decentralized social groups provide an environment in which social order and cohesion may be maintained by mores and primary-group controls. Sandstone, the "name of an estate in Topanga, California, which was the site of an extended experiment in open sexuality," provides an example. In *More Joy* Comfort reflects on his visit to Sandstone:

On several nights a week there was open house for 400 or so couples who were members. On some of these occasions visitors brought their own food, but on Saturdays an excellent, buffet-style dinner was provided, and visitors might stay overnight. The pattern on Wednesdays was similar but the numbers (often as many as 50 on a Saturday) much smaller. Sunbathing and the hot pool were always available. Nudity was general, but neither that nor anything else except ordinarily civilized behavior was obligatory—a structure without rules was maintained by the general mores of the group. Open sexual expression of any kind was allowed anywhere (except on the front lawn, after a police helicopter nearly crashed while observing it). Drugs and minors were banned, and alcohol not greatly encouraged. (p. 160)

Mores largely determine behavior. But not all mores are of equal value. Those at work at Sandstone were the product of a highly intelligent and politically, as well as sexually, liberated group. The creation of a noncoercive society, Comfort's works imply, involves the selective retention of those mores which contribute most to species survival.

In contrast to the Hobbesian notion of the social contract resulting from the brutal war of each against all, Comfort advocates the modern sociological conclusion that man "is a social animal—the basis of his social behavior is the family group, and the chief regulator of his behavior is custom" (*Nature and Human Nature*, p. 17). His background in primatology allows him, however, to go beyond both behaviorist and sociological theories. Man is a "social animal" not simply because he has been culturally conditioned to be so, but because he possesses as well innate predispositions towards sociability. Skinner, who places inordinate emphasis on environment in explaining behavior, "has no computer experience," Comfort believes, "and I think Skinner tends to regard the mind as *tabula rasa* on which environment writes. Well, I don't think this is entirely true. This is a mechanistic view. To put it in automation terms, the brain is an evolved system which has been evolved already in response to the environment in evolution. And it's like a student's answer book which has got the spaces for the answers to be written in."[39]

Part of what is written in may be a tendency towards mutual assistance. Desmond Morris writes of "mutual aid" or "mutual assistance"—"the basic biological urge to co-operate with our fellow men"—as a fundamental prerequisite for the survival of man in a hostile environment.[40] The concept of mutual aid is indepted to Peter Kropotkin, both ethologist and anarchist theorist, who posited the concept of mutual aid or species solidarity as a primary mechanism in biological evolution; his *Mutual Aid* (1902) counterbalances nineteenth-century notions about the "survival of the fittest." Like Morris, Comfort in *Sex in Society* argues for "both 'togetherness' and technology, both mutual aid and modern medicine" (p. 169). Morris's view of mutual aid is oversimplified inasmuch as it does not adequately acknowledge the role of learning in fostering mutual aid among animals and men. Comfort is to be distinguished from writers popularizing ethological ideas, such as Morris, Robert Ardrey, and Konrad Lorenz, in that he emphasizes that behavior generally is dominated by conditioning: "The social override, the learned override, is huge; and with this I would always agree with Skinner."[41]

The apparent antithesis of mutual aid, intrapsecies aggression, is for Comfort also largely a socially conditioned response. Asocial, centralized society, a cause of psychological disorders, is also a major cause of violence. "It seems to be universally agreed by primatologists," Comfort writes in *Nature and Human Nature*, "that healthy wild primates almost *never* fight within the species; even the strict dominance we see in some species is established by a kind of behavioural consent, not by violence. But primates confined or stressed do exhibit the kind of aggression, often pointless, which we see in human hooligans, politicians and delinquents (I am not being sarcastic). Either Man differs in this respect from all other primates, or aggressive and destructive behaviour is a sign of stress, of one kind or another, in him too" (p. 148). Similarly, Morris, citing the stresses of centralization as one cause of antisocial behavior, argues that " 'the law forbids men to do only what the artificial conditions of civilization drive them to do.' " But Morris, analyzing the development of the "super tribe," notes than an " 'isolating law' " functions in the "super tribe" to hold it together: "it gives cohesion to a society by providing it with a unique identity."[42] Custom, language, religion, and war—"nothing ties tighter the in-group bonds than an out-group threat"—are also cohesive forces that help "to bind the members of a super-tribe together. . . ."[43] The function of law in general in controlling behavior in centralized society in which anonymity isolates the individual from primary-group controls is accepted by most sociologists. Comfort's dissatisfaction with law or coercive control is linked to his dissatisfaction with centralization or with what Morris describes as the "super tribe."

More carefully than Morris, Lorenz, and Ardrey, Comfort stresses the multidimensional character of agression (see *More Joy,* pp. 100–107). His works generally imply that assertion of personality against an inhibiting and hostile environment is a legitimate form of aggressive behavior. Furthermore, some forms of aggression—in particular, hostility—may be discharged in sexual play. Lorenz, who believes in the possibility of sublimating inbuilt aggressiveness, argues for sports. Comfort, who in *Sex in Society* views sexual intercourse as "the healthiest and most important human sport" (p. 26), has recently noted that sexual play is "a way of exorcising some" of our aggressions "in the way that child play is. I'm only taking it [sex] as the most important form of adult play. Children do play bang-you're-dead games with each other. What they learn by them is that their hostile feelings don't destroy other people and don't cause other people to go away. Everybody needs this awareness. And a certain amount of hostility is, I think, naturally in sex in order to avoid a takeover by the other person, particularly in our society where we have been encouraged to think that one ought to take over another person. . . . George Barker, as you know, teaches men and women to fight with batacas and pillow-fight. But in fact if you watch this they may start by displaying some hostility, but it ends as playfulness, and finally they end up in bed."[44] Unlike Lorenz and Ardrey, Comfort does not believe that most people are "loaded with agression. They may be loaded with the fear of it."[45] Sexual play is, among other things, a means of overcoming such fear.

Play behavior in general is for Comfort a cohesive force. Kropotkin notes that play behavior in animals is a manifestation "of an excess of forces—'the joy of life,' and a desire to communicate in some way or another with other inidividuals of the same or other species—in short, a manifestation of sociability proper. . . ."[46] Like Kropotkin and later ethologists, Comfort sees animal play as a "form of training" as well as including "mere ebullience like that of the dolphins or the otter." He also concludes,

As such it is most evident in social and semi-social animals, and most evident of all in Man. Play, which joins hands with art on one hand, through makebelieve, and with love on the other (since play with a sexual partner and with children are two of the most psychologically important kinds), is another human-primate socializing force in which we can express and discharge emotion without prejudice to serious purposes. (*Nature and Human Nature,* p. 190)

Play, art, work, religion, and sexuality are all socializing forces, Comfort believes (see *Nature and Human Nature,* chapter nine).

Religion, in its archetypal rather than institutional and theological sense, is socializing inasmuch as it is relational or fusional. In this sense it is analogous to sexuality and may involve or use an identical neurological mechanism. In "Notes on the Biology of Religion" (1975), Comfort argues that "the mechanism of the 'oceanic experience' itself," like the ecstatic or fusional experience of sexuality, possibly "uses the wiring of, the reward of orgasm."[47] In 1974 Comfort stated that religion would probably continue to exist in a sexually liberated society, but it "would be a sexualized religion." Where religious experiences "were only substitutions for sexuality," they would possibly come to be perceived as "inferior to the real thing. But where they had other connotations," such as "other ways of delimiting ego boundaries," those "might well be accessory to, or in addition to, or might be reached through the experiences one had in sexuality." "The interesting thing about Sandstone," Comfort also observed, "was, the experience felt much more religious than it felt horny. . . . You couldn't have anything less like a brothel." Sandstone is "sexual, but it's also an intense experience of relationship. I didn't expect that. I thought it would be fun. But I didn't think it would work like that, but it does."[48] Such observations foreshadow his more developed reflections in "Notes on the Biology of Religion":

But in general we are here referring to an ingrained and very early character of human attempts at ego-boundary manipulation, that they are social, or communal, that they produce both insight and bonding between the inseers, and that the two feed each other. No human being is so sophisticated as to be quite unsusceptible to this sociopsychologic process: very emancipated people find unexpected reassurance in group nakedness, and the Greek philosophers, hardly the most superstitious or credulous of people, found a profound peak experience in the Eleusinian Mysteries.

Delimiting ego-boundaries, without sacrificing individuality and personal responsibility, involves acquiring a new sense of one's relationship with persons, objects, and the archetypal dimensions of the mind—the "structure of human inner space."[49] In this sense also it is related to the relational as well as self-exploratory characteristics of sexuality: "The more you feel at one with yourself as a functioning organism," Comfort noted in 1974, "the more you feel—this sort of feeling of eroticized benevolence extends to society and to inanimate objects."[50]

Such "religious" experience as that which Comfort experienced at Sandstone, as well as religious experience generally, is for Comfort without metaphysical implications. Archetypal patterns, accordingly, are not indications of a transcendent supernatural order. Rather, they are internal because neurologically imprinted, although reinforced and shaped by environmental experiences:

The structures discovered with such excitement by William Yeats in occultism and in his wife's trances, the matter of folklore and myth, the "group unconscious" of Jung, and the esoterica now in revival which so excite the nonlinear minded are not arbitrary and vain imaginings. Misleading they undoubtedly are if we take them literally. What they represent is the playback, not of external pattern, but of the structure of our pattern-selecting mechanism.

How this mechanism is situated in respect to the wiring of the "I" experience is at present anybody's guess. We have a "group unconscious," not in the sense of an intraspecific form of ESP, but as all IBM computers of the same model have a "group unconscious," some aspects of which reflect software, some hardware wiring, and yet others the geometry of hole-spacing in punch cards; in other words it is structural, and it is the structure through and with which the homuncular "I" looks out, and the structure it sees as zero-input display when it attempts to look in.[51]

By contrast conventional religion takes its mythology literally, as if actually external. It also projects internalized parental and social conscience and dominance (involving pecking-order awareness) into the real or imagined environment: "humans project dominance out into the nonhuman because it controls and can surprise or threaten them by its initiatives. . . ."⁵²

The socializing character of sexuality per se is for Comfort of greater significance than that of religion. In *Nature and Human Nature* he writes:

> What then, is the answer, and what, if any, are the social and mental forces which can make humans fully social, give them the power of joy without limiting their capacity for necessary sorrow, and enable them to be free of anxiety without blinking the facts of the human situation? Philosophy, religion, religious and stoical resignation have all been prescribed. Oddly enough—or perhaps not so oddly—the psychiatric evidence seems now, in many people's view, to point to the same force which socialized primates, made us able to live in families, and motivated our personal and social behaviour, namely sexual love—extended, through the peculiar role it has come to play in human economy, far outside its original context of the desire to copulate, and made more similar to the poet Schiller's idea of "joy"; a sexual affection, carrying the same pleasurable intensity we find in man-woman relations, but spilling over into all types of relationship, even our relationship with things. Some may feel that psychiatrists and poets are both enthusiasts who have sex on the brain, and may wish to cry "Steady!" at this point. Primatologists, however, cannot be justly subject to these suspicions—and it is from the primatologists that this concept of "eros" (love transmuted into love-of-living and love-for-your neighbour) now draws most of its support. (p. 182)

Similar conclusions on the possibility of civilization derived from "free libidinal relations" rather than from "repressive sublimation" are at work in Herbert Marcuse's *Eros and Civilization*.⁵³ Comfort mentions Marcuse in "Sexuality in a Zero Growth Society" (1974): "Marcuse, in discussing the 'erotization of relationships' as a political force was once challenged to 'go erotize the state of Kansas.' My suggestion is that this may in fact be happening."⁵⁴ But Marcuse, a Marxist and no primatologist, lacks adequate credentials to be scientifically convincing. "Until one sees it in its primate context, the idea of erotizing the world looks like eyewash, or, to a hard-boiled Freudian, regression to the boundless self-centredness of infancy" (*Nature and Human Nature*, p. 200).

Comfort's understanding of the primate context is probably indebted to Solly Zuckerman who argues in his highly regarded *The Social Life of Monkeys and Apes* (1932) that the "main factor that determines social grouping in sub-human primates is sexual attraction."[55] With the emergence in evolution of year-round female receptivity to the male, permanent associations become possible: "The factors underlying associations of monkeys and apes are characterized by their continuous, rather than intermittent, sexual nature," according to Zuckerman.[56] Later primatologists echo Zuckerman's conclusions. In "The Origin of Society," Marshall Sahlins writes that "among subhuman primates sex had organized society. . . ."[57] In his classic "A Field Study in Siam of the Behavior and Social Relations of the Gibbon," C. R. Carpenter concludes that because there is apparently no "definite breeding season" in gibbons, "copulation may reinforce the male-female bond throughout the year."[58] Such associations in gibbons, structured around the pair-bond, "form the core of the group."[59] In *Nature and Human Nature* Comfort, citing Carpenter for his knowledge of gibbon social life, applies such conclusions to the human condition. The emergence of continuous female receptivity, an "apparently trifling change in behavior," was "probably the trigger, or one of the triggers, which set off the evolution of Man." The function of sex in the evolving human species, moreover, was "social," an "expression of 'togetherness' between mates, or of play, or of the requirement for physical pleasure" (p. 19).

But primate societies do not cohere simply on the basis of heterosexual attraction. Sahlins notes that "sex is more than a force of attraction between adult males and females; it also operates among the young and between individuals of the same sex. . . . And while we might deem some of the forms perversions, to a monkey or an ape they are all just sociable."[60] Following Freud, Sahlins goes on to observe that the development of culture involved the surbordination of the "sex drives to the needs of the group."[61] In his later works Comfort views homosexual impulses at the human, as well as at the primate, level as possibly productive of coherence. If they are, they have species survival value, and, hence, may have been fostered in evolution by natural selection: "Homosexual potentialities quite possibly enable us to become functionally social, by giving the male group, which cuts across pair-mating family structure, the steam necessary for it to perform. In other words, these 'abnormalities' are or were probably adaptive, at least as potentialities—that in large doses they upset reproduction is beside the point: social insects have evolved wholly sterile individuals."[62] Apparently influenced by the ideas of earlier primatologists, his views on homosexuality have undergone modification. In *Barbarism and Sexual Freedom* Comfort writes of male homosexuality as "probably, though not certainly, propagated by war . . ." (p. 20). Homosexuality, in other words, may be primarily the consequence of existence in asocial society as well as of female-excluding military life. In *Sex in Society* he argues that "homosexual impulses exist *potentially* in almost all males. . ." (p. 23). Although continuing to recognize that exclusively homosexual behavior may be partially propagated by environmental causes, in *More Joy* Comfort writes that homosexual impulses are an "unused potential present in all straight men which they've trodden on under orders from society" (p. 111).

The traditional anarchist view of history, as noted earlier, is similar to that expressed by Christian mythology: Eden, expulsion into a period of conflict with the demonic authority of secular society, and Paradise regained. Such a tripartite view of history comes to assume a new mythological dimension in Comfort's later works under the direction of his developing view of Eros as productive of social cohesion. Interpreted from Comfort's perspective, what has come to be known as "the sexual revolution" may involve a rediscovering of forgotten or repressed potentialities. Sociologically, movement towards sexual liberalization may mean rediscovering some of the potentialities for social living of primate societies and some primitive, "matriform" societies. Psychologically, movement towards sexual freedom may mean rediscovering some of the potentialities of childhood, such as playfulness, spontaneity, and the capacity for libidinal gratification generally. Both the development of adulthood and patriarchal society involve a "fall," in Christian as well as early Romantic mythology, into a condition governed by the internalization of the values of the father or father surrogates. In biblical myth, Adam repents and learns obedience. Such a condition involves as well the inhibition of libidinal gratification in the name of necessity. The pleasure principle is replaced by the reality principle, or, in biblical myth, Adam is forced to live by the sweat of his brow. In *Nature and Human Nature* Comfort argues that

Eden is not a historic state but a human potentiality, and there are societies which have come close to realizing it, giving to all their activities the undifferentiated libidinal zest we see in young children. This is a primate ability in contrast to the dominance-society of baboon days: oddly enough it is the industrial, acquisitive revolution, which saw our own society at its most baboon-like, which has put us in reach of realizing the Edenic and unbaboon-like potentialities of our other socio-sexual selves by removing the compulsion to hard, compulsory and acquisitive work. "Free" societies are ebullient or gentle, but not "hard-working" in the competitive sense. (p. 189)

Among contemporary societies Comfort may have in mind the essentially nonauthoritarian, noncompetitive, unacquisitive, gentle, and maternal Arapesh made famous by Margaret Mead.

The function of Eros as productive of social cohesion, but not its primatological basis, appears early in Comfort's works. His early views are more simply Freudian. Freud in *An Outline of Psychoanalysis* writes of the erotic instincts which work "to combine organic substances into ever greater unities and to preserve them thus—in short, to bind them together."[63] In *Barbarism and Sexual Freedom* (1948) Comfort observes that the "sexual impulse, whether we regard it as the Eros of Freud or as a force of purely biochemical status (they are not mutually exclusive) is in itself so essential a manifestation of this species-solidarity [i.e., mutual aid or cooperation and cohesion in a species], and of the attempt and will to survive, that its submergence or diversion is a danger-signal in any society" (p. 3). And in *Authority and Delinquency* (1950) he writes of an "incentive-mechanism" (as powerful as religion), within the "human activities of love and home-making; these are the key determinants of cultural pattern . . ." (p. 124). The primatological context becomes clear after correlations between animal and human behavior become commonplace in the works of Lorenz and other ethologists. But Kropotkin had already demonstrated in writing *Mutual Aid* that ethological observations had applicability to the struggle against coercive society.

CHAPTER 2

The Early Novels

T HE significance of Comfort as a novelist has been the subject of
wide differences of opinion. Whereas reviews of individual
novels have often been unfavorable, serious literary criticism has
consistently called attention to Comfort as an artist possessing significant intellectual and imaginative abilities. For example, Henry
Treece in *How I See Apocalypse* praises Comfort's remarkable ability
to create novels "around incidents and in scenery of which he can only
have an imaginative knowledge. . . ."[1] Harold Drasdo in "Alex
Comfort's Art and Scope" concludes that Comfort's novels are

without exception . . . exciting as stories. Their inhabitants represent a range
of class and nationality which few contemporary novelists can match. Yet
these characters are neither national stereotypes nor uprooted cosmopoli-
tans; they are steeped in their own cultures and if they become international
or extranational in outlook it is when reason or experience has forced it.[2]

In *The Freedom of Poetry* Derek Stanford argues that *The Power
House*, Comfort's most popular novel, is one of the "two most
important novels published in England during the 'war' " (the other
being Koestler's *Arrival and Departure*).[3] P. H. Newby observes in
The Novel: 1945–1950,

Throughout the nineteenth century the typical English novelist seemed to
survey the panorama of life from the depths of a comfortable armchair and he
passed comments on the scene with kindness and confidence. In the twentieth century this is no longer possible, any complacency that existed has
been swept away, and it is obvious that the young writer must think as he has
never thought before. Alex Comfort gives the best evidence of such thinking
among the novelists who have emerged in recent years and it is the quality of
thought in *The Power House,* and a later novel *On This Side Nothing,* which
gives them their distinction.[4]

As an artist, Comfort has apparently distributed his efforts primarily between his poetry and novels. That he took seriously his role as a novelist is indicated in part by the fact that the novel is the only genre to which Comfort dedicated an extended study, *The Novel and Our Time* (1948).

His views on the moral function of the novel are traditional in the sense that they imply a dual function for art, the union of Horace's *dulce* and *utile*. In the context of the 1940s, however, his views may be seen as approximating those of Sartre who advocates commitment or engagement on the part of artists with respect to moral and political problems and a rejection of art for art's sake theories and practices. In *The Novel and Our Time* Comfort argues that the artist, rather than escaping "into the contemplation of pure form" (he cites, later, Joyce's *Finnegans Wake* as an example), should "consciously assume responsibility for his humanity" (p. 21), and that

no form of art can be regarded in isolation from the society in which the artist lives, and it is only comparatively recently in history that critics and readers have come to regard artistic activities as a separate branch of endeavour, similar to one of the branches of technology. Characteristic literary forms are only brought into existence by bodies of people who live, and to some extent think, along the same lines and in the same general pattern. At the present time the entire literary endeavour of "serious" writers, with very few exceptions, and over a very wide area of the world, is divided unequally between the novel and lyrical poetry, with a commercial preponderance in favour of the novel. There are subsidiary reasons for this choice, including the financial advantages of fiction and the renewed technical resources of poetry, but the main incentive to novel writing is, for most of us, the fact that the novel is the readiest and most acceptable way of embodying ideas and artistic statements in the context of our time. (p. 9)

In implicit contrast to the neocritical emphasis on the novel as a self-enclosed art object, Comfort emphasizes the practical necessity for the modern novelist's creation of self-contained works of art. The disappearance of universally accepted moral and philosophical assumptions necessitates such a mode of creation:

The novelist to-day has to cut himself off from any basic assumptions, and in doing so he must be capable of presenting the entire canvas which he selects in a framework of a coherent vision which is very nearly explanatory. Futhermore, this "major" vision must be infinitely more clear-cut than its equivalent in music or painting, because literature expresses explicit ideas. A far greater strain falls on this cohering or synthetic aptitude in the novelist, and on the other essential attribute which goes with it, responsibility. (pp. 18–19)

For Comfort "embodying ideas," or expressing "explicit ideas," means creating works of art which express a coherent moral vision, as well as including philosophical ideas, some of which he has articulated—or is to articulate—in prose elsewhere, in the medium of the novel. In this sense his art resembles that of Sartre, Huxley, or Shaw. John Doheny classifies Comfort as a "novelist of ideas," comparing him with E. M. Forster and Sterne.[5] The classification seems appropriate to much of Comfort's fiction as long as it is not assumed, as in R. C. Churchill's essay on the "comedy of ideas," that the "novel of ideas" in the twentieth century is in "the English tradition of comedy, both in its admirable detail and its casual sprawl. . . ."[6] The concept of "novelist of ideas," broadly interpreted, or philosophical novelist, is useful to the extent that it allows the critic to see a common tradition underlying the novels of Comfort, Sartre, Camus, Dostoevski, Santayana, Godwin, Chesterton, Butler, Orwell, Huxley, and others. Such a tradition has roots in the Classical dialogue and Neoclassical imitations (such as those of Hume), the philosophical fable (for example, More's *Utopia,* Bacon's *New Atlantis,* Johnson's *Rasselas,* Voltaire's *Candide),* and the fiction of Rousseau *(The New Héloïse* and *Emile).*

Northrop Frye in his *Anatomy of Criticism* observes that the "forms of prose fiction are mixed" and provides narrower classifications which have some applicability to Comfort's fiction. Frye argues that when we are reading Huxley's novels, as well as Rousseau's *Emile,* Voltaire's *Candide,* and Butler's *The Way of All Flesh,* "we feel that we are turning from the novel" to "another form of fiction": "The form used by these authors is the Menippean satire" which "deals less with people as such than with mental attitudes." On the other hand, Joyce's *Portrait,* which also includes abstract theories, owes a debt, Frye notes, to "another tradition of prose fiction," the confession which "flows into the novel," the mixture producing "the fictional autobiography, the *Künstler-roman,* and kindred types."[7] Confessional elements are at work in several of Comfort's novels, particularly *No Such Liberty,* and the devices of characterization in *A Giant's Strength* and *Come Out to Play,* as well as the atmosphere of

Come Out to Play, have much in common with that of Menippean satire.

Huxley in *Point Counter Point* has Philip Quarles write in his notebook that the "chief defect of the novel of ideas is that you must write about people who have ideas to express—which excludes all but about .01 per cent. of the human race."[8] Not understood as a "defect" by Comfort, or by most philosophical novelists, Quarles's, or Huxley's, generalization partially explains, at any rate, Comfort's selection of protagonists who are usually intellectuals. Unlike Huxley's protagonists, however, they are usually not bookish personalities interested in analyzing, alluding to, refuting, or elaborating upon the theories of others. In this respect, Comfort's protagonists are much less complicated than Huxley's, and the manner in which they express their ideas is usually simpler and closer to the level of ordinary conversation.

The pattern of salvation in the novels of Huxley, Sterne, Dostoevski, and Barth consists of characters whose intellectualization of their problems, with an accompanying augmentation of their discomfiture, points towards the realization that salvation is not to be found in reason, but, if found at all, in modes of being which transcend rational analysis. Comfort's characters usually move from unthinking, mentally distorted acquiescence in collective unreason to quest after and find salvation—with varying degrees of success—in intellectual clarification: redemption in the development of reason and understanding, intellectual order in the midst of the external anarchy of collective psychopathology.

What may be said to be the general mythical development of the narrative corresponding to such development within characters is: movement from a modern version of Bunyan's City of Destruction, or Dante's Inferno—the urban, military orders depicted in *No Such Liberty, The Power House, On This Side Nothing* and *A Giant's Strength*—to experience purgation and discover inward salvation while pilgrimaging, as refugees, through a European wasteland being devastated by war in *No Such Liberty, The Power House,* and *On This Side Nothing,* or pilgrimaging within a literal wasteland, a desert, in *A Giant's Strength.* To the extent that the revolutionary philosophies reached by Comfort's protagonists have apocalyptic and utopian meanings or implications, they are provided a beatific inward vision of the new Jerusalem—the counterpart in Comfort's realistic fiction of the apocalyptic implications at work at the conclusion of his *Cities of the Plain* as well as in some of his poetry.

I   No Such Liberty

Reviewing Alfred Lomnitz's *Never Mind, Mr. Lom* in *Life and Letters Today* (1941), Comfort observes that "we are likely to see a good many books by men who experienced the internment camps of militant Democracy during 1941," and goes on to add: "there is room here for a really great book."[9] *No Such Liberty* (1941) represents a response by Comfort to the possibilities inherent in the neglected, unpopular subject of Allied mistreatment of aliens. The novel's narrator, Dr. Helmut Breitz, flees political persecution in Germany where he has worked in Cologne as a pathologist, but finds that he is not immune from political persecution on English soil. Because of his pacifist beliefs, he is classified as a class B alien, and subsequently committed to an English internment camp. Eventually released and given permission to emigrate to America, he is haunted, at the novel's conclusion, by the fear that the wave of political hysteria from which he and his wife have suffered "will have reached America before we can leave and we shall have our ordeal over again" (p. 248). The title alludes to the narrator's imprisonment and suggests, more generally, that a sense of personal powerlessness and negation is to be a dominant motif of the narrative.

George Orwell, in a review for *Adelphi* (1941), observes that *No Such Liberty* is "a good novel as novels go at this moment," but, noting that "all writing nowadays is propaganda," finds that Comfort's novel is propaganda for a bad cause: "The notion that you can somehow defeat violence by submitting to it is simply a flight from fact." According to Orwell,

Civilisation rests ultimately on coercion. What holds society together is not the policeman but the goodwill of common men, and yet that goodwill is powerless unless the policeman is there to back it up. Any government which refused to use violence in its own defence would cease almost immediately to exist, because it could be overthrown by any body of men, or even any individual, that was less scrupulous. Objectively, whoever is not on the side of the policeman is on the side of the criminal, and vice versa. In so far as it hampers the British war effort, British pacifism is on the side of the Nazis, and German pacifism, if it exists, is on the side of Britain and the USSR. Since pacifists have more freedom of action in countries where traces of democracy survive, pacifism can act more effectively against democracy than for it. Objectively the pacifist is pro-Nazi.[10]

Orwell concludes his review by observing,

There is no such thing as neutrality in this war. The whole population of the world is involved in it, from the Eskimos to the Andamanese, and since one must inevitably help one side or the other, it is better to know what one is doing and count the cost. Men like Darlan and Laval have at any rate had the courage to make their choice and proclaim it openly. The New Order, they say, must be established at all costs, and "il faut écra bouiller l'Angleterre." Mr. Murry appears, at any rate at moments, to think likewise. The Nazis, he says, are "doing the dirty work of the Lord" (they certainly did an exceptionally dirty job when they attacked Russia), and we must be careful "lest in fighting against Hitler we are fighting against God." Those are not pacifist sentiments, since if carried to their logical conclusion they involve not only surrendering to Hitler but helping him in his various forthcoming wars, but they are at least straightforward and courageous. I do not myself see Hitler as the saviour, even the unconscious saviour, of humanity, but there is a strong case for thinking him so, far stronger than most people in England imagine. What there is no case for is to denounce Hitler and at the same time look down your nose at the people who actually keep you out of his clutches. That is simply a highbrow variant of British hypocrisy, a product of capitalism in decay, and the sort of thing for which Europeans, who at any rate understand the nature of a policeman and a dividend, justifiably despise us.[11]

Whatever may be the marginal philosophical merits of Orwell's criticisms, they have the practical effect of underscoring the subversive character of *No Such Liberty*. Recognizing Dr. Breitz as a spokesman for some of Comfort's pacifist ideas, Orwell also concludes that *No Such Liberty* is "autobiographical, not in the sense that the events described in it have actually happened, but in the sense that the author identifies himself with the hero, thinks him worthy of sympathy and agrees with the sentiments that he expresses."[12] Robert Callahan, on the other hand, finds Orwell's statement of the relationship between Comfort and Dr. Breitz to be "thoroughly misleading." Callahan views Breitz as an "authoritarian personality," as a type of "scapegoat, or 'passive barbarian,' as Mumford would call him," an "emblem of his society" and a "typical citizen of the 'telephone exchange' society."[13]

Callahan's view of Breitz is correct with respect to the first part of the novel, but misleading to the extent that it fails to take into account the degree and rapidity of Breitz's progress from unthinking acquiescence in collective unreason to a state of intellectual clarification. There are no heroes and no villains in Comfort's early novels, and Breitz's state at the novel's conclusion, a defeated man who confesses that his "desire for liberty" has been "smashed" by his "days in prison" (p. 237), is not to be taken as a model to be emulated. But he does develop a significant degree of insight concerning the immoral and destructive character of authoritarian society. It is the influence exerted by his wife's example of political responsibility—she has helped to smuggle young men out of Germany and has helped to write a pamphlet "which appealed to the mothers of Germany"—and Braunstein's perceptive explanation of the character and causes of fascism which are largely responsible for Breitz's moral development.

Shortly after arriving at the Central (hospital), Breitz and Dr. Braunstein, the director of the Central, discuss the political situation in Germany. When Braunstein asks Breitz what his "diagnosis" is, Breitz professes ignorance, but is willing to put forth the hypothesis that "quite a lot of it seems to be sheer discontent with all the footlers we've had in the past . . ." (p. 21). Braunstein, in turn, observes that fascism in Germany has its origin in a national sense of impotence. Individuals, Braunstein goes on to argue, are also motivated to struggle for power or dominance because of a corresponding sense of personal inferiority. Such views on the origins of the psychopathology of power parallel those developed in Erich Fromm's *The Fear of Freedom,* published in the same year as *No Such Liberty.* They also seemingly reflect the psychological theories of Adler on the function of a sense of inferiority as a primary motive in human interactions:

"We're afraid, Dr. Breitz. We're a scared, silly nation. We've lost our faith in ourselves ever since we saw those men come home beaten. Now we're scared. We daren't be weak for fear of being imposed on. We daren't be decent for fear of seeming weak. We're scared of the English, of the Jews, of each other—those oafs in uniform who go round throwing bricks in windows had rickets when they were children. They're undersized, and they bully and go about in gangs to make up for it." (p. 22)

Callahan sees Breitz as showing only "the beginning of awareness into what the novel itself is expressing about the real nature of a society motivated by fear" as late as page 201 of the novel (in chapter eighteen). He argues also that Braunstein's knowledge "that society has become demonic" is "lost on Breitz." Both Breitz and Burwell, according to Callahan, do not belong to the type that "manifests some insight into the human psychic processes through which the real world becomes an 'unreal' nightmare."[14] As we might expect, Breitz's knowledge of the extent of social psychopathology continues to develop after he arrives in England. However, while still in

Germany and early in his stay in England, Breitz manifests a relatively high degree of insight into the character of social irresponsibility.

In chapter seven he employs Braunstein's descriptive phrase defining German fascism as "a pathological process" (p. 23) in describing the mass psychopathology of an amorphous assembly of Nazis and Nazi supporters (which he observes while seeking his wife, who herself is being sought by the Gestapo). He also perceptively observes that dehumanization and a loss of individual power and autonomy are significant features of such a "pathological process":

> In that audience not a man was master of himself. A pathological process. I'd never seen a crowd carried away so. As we skirted the square, at each street we crossed, we came in sight of the shores of that great black lake. Figures were crawling up the statue and the trees like ants out of a flood, and the whole lake was tossing and throwing up crests while the torches reeled and winked. They were chanting in unison now, and the whole mass began to pour in a viscous stream down the Sebengebirgeplatz. We saw them in flashes down the streets we passed across. (p. 67)

After he arrives in England and hears of the Belgium debacle, Breitz cynically alludes to the "slow and painful death of a civilization," but turns from such depressing thoughts to contemplate the birth of his son. (Callahan, assuming that Breitz lacks "insight," argues that his observation about civilization "seems to have been motivated by [Comfort's] impatience with the obtuseness of his protagonist."[15]) In chapter ten, while recuperating in England from his harrowing and debilitating experiences in escaping from Germany, Breitz observes that a similar pathological process to the one he had seen near the Sebengebirgeplatz in Germany is at work in England. His description and subsequent evaluation reflect, in both phraseology and substance, the influence of Braunstein's early analysis concerning "fear" and weakness as motives for social pathology. But he is now in a position to move beyond Braunstein's analysis by generalizing it. Breitz realizes that English political and military authoritarianism is not potentially different from the forms of fascism against which England is engaged in military conflict:

> As I grew better, and was able to walk to the sun room unaided, Anna used to come in often to tell me about the world outside, and my heart sank, because I realised that the same fear was moving here as in Germany, the fear of being weak, of adhering to right principles lest they should not be an

expedient, practical policy—to make any concession, for fear of defeat. . . .
  I knew that all the talk of strength I heard . . . were the same as the assurances that I'd left plastered on the complaining walls of Cologne by the Rhine, and that they'd blossom the same things—injustice and enormity. It's not that you of London are evil; it's not that the infection has gone so far that you beat and jail men, individual men, who tell you that the bacteria of your disease are there. But they are there. And I know that they must, and they will grow, till you are as we, and fear has redoubled itself. (pp. 108–109)

Before the English judge who is to determine his status as an alien, Breitz naively expects from English justice more than he is to receive. But his answers to the judge concerning his political beliefs constitute an indictment of power—"force and intimidation"—as a fundamental and perennial cause of human suffering. Brought up as a Lutheran, Breitz answers the judge's questions concerning his political philosophy by defining himself politically as a Christian:

"Dr. Breitz, what do you call yourself politically?"
"How do you mean?"
"I mean, Socialist, Liberal, Marxist, no party?"
"I'm a Christian."
"Yes, I know. But your politics?"
"Politically, I'm a Christian."
"But that isn't a political policy."
"It is the only one I recognise," I said. "It involves the belief that force and intimidation aggravate evil, and love tends to overcome it by suffering."
"I don't quite follow you," said the judge. "But to return to what you said just now, would you advocate surrender to the people who've nearly killed you?"
"No. But if they ask my opinion I must give it."
"But it would mean death for yourself and thousands like you."
"I know, but it's not the first time the disease has killed the physician."
"You're prepared for that?"
"I hope I am."
"Then why did you run away from Germany?"
I didn't know. (pp. 141–42)

Inasmuch as England is professedly Christian, the dialogue between Breitz and the English judge contributes to the novel's analysis of the disparity between appearance and reality by undercutting the hypocrisy and inconsistency of Christianized England's involvement in the war. Breitz's answers also display the unstable combination in his personality of insight and simplicity. But he is not answering the

English judge by rationalizing "slaughter in the name of peace and love," as Callahan suggests.[16] He is not advocating surrender or victory. (Later in the novel, when Breitz hears of the Belgian debacle, he contemplates English "Defeat or victory," but knows that neither "would bear thinking upon," for the "first was death for me and Anna—the second for our son.") Breitz is advocating a mode of spiritual existence which makes either surrender or victory fundamentally superfluous. He is, admittedly, too passive (as compared, for example, with his wife), too ready to play the role of suffering servant. But he is also the first of Comfort's protagonists to recognize that violence cannot be counteracted with violence. His Christian pacifism may be modeled after that of the Christian anarchist Tolstoy who argues in *The Kingdom of God Is Within You* that a Christian, by enduring violence, "not only frees himself from all external power, but the world also."[17]

Like Tolstoy, Breitz defines his Christianity largely in ethical terms rather than as a matter of doctrine. What may be said to be the fundamental doctrinal aspects of his Christianity are similar to the secular ethics at the heart of Comfort's own philosophy. Before Bretiz's conversation with the English judge and immediately after explaining to Burwell that "military defeat" has become an obsession with the Germans, Breitz reflects:

> When I discuss politics with medical men I am always ill at ease. I think that of all the secular professions ours has the deepest insight into the troubles of man. You cannot walk through a hospital without meeting the three unfashionable, but permanent snags in human affairs, decay, fear, and original sin. There is a stage when you see them and study them in others. Then there is a stage when you see them and are aghast at them in yourself. And then, before you can do anything for the patients of that hospital, you require a philosophy. And the only philosophy which is prepared to recognise the proportions of all three of your adversaries is Christianity. (p. 114)

Two years after the publication of *No Such Liberty* Comfort (in *Life and Letters Today*) lists a belief in "Original Sin" as one of the defining doctrines of the New Romanticism:

> One of [the] principles or properties common to humanity is the congenital inability not to abuse power when incorporated into any sort of body. This is roughly speaking the doctrine of Original Sin, but it has no mystical basis and there is no corresponding doctrine of Grace. . . . [Our political attitude] owes something, but not much, to the corresponding Calvinism of Niebuhr and

Karl Barth, and it recognizes a penetrating allegorical statement of the impasse in Genesis, where man's inability to live up to his principles is made to coincide with the discovery of the principles themselves. But this is not in any sense a religious belief. [18]

No Such Liberty anticipates Comfort's later novels, especially *The Power House*, in its application of cinematographic techniques. For example, the opening paragraph, a flashback, begins by combining what may be said to be a zoom technique with a gothic, nightmarish atmosphere, somewhat after the manner of *Citizen Kane*. It proceeds by panning for a panoramic effect in order to show that the Central hospital is the center of Cologne; for life begins, ends, and has its being in the Central:

Sometimes, when I can sleep, I dream of the day I returned to the Central. It stood there at the corner of the Glockenstrasse, just as ugly and as pretentious as I had left it, with its red brick frontage, its preposterous clock tower, and the row of sham Greek columns in yellow sandstone round its upper floors. Between those columns the tall windows were open, and I could see the black enamelled rails of the patients' beds, and the brilliant red and black stripes of the regulation blankets. Some of the inmates were hidden behind news-papers, while others, their faces very pink and clean against the hospital linen, were lying back sleeping, in strange attitudes, like a nest of young animals suddenly uncovered. I could see their round black mouths open— others were sitting, gazing straight out across the miscellany of roofs by the riverside to the tall spidery bridges, the tower of the Rhein Museum and the grey haze over the river. The cathedral stood away to the right, the Central's only competitor along the westward skyline, like a gigantic sitting rabbit, its two spires pointing upward for ears, and its short body hunched behind them. Among it all the Central stood like a middle-aged, pretentious midwife, with glass-roofed clinics and wooden turntable huts for the con-sumptives all about her feet, among the tenement houses along the riverside. It was the Central that mended and manufactured all the inhabitants for those miles of similar red streets with their blackened plane trees, whose houses ran up and down the banks of the Rhine like the semi-quavers of a cadenza passage. There was a big ugly sky sign opposite the Outpatients, which said, "Ganz Koln trinkt Carlsberg." That was very nearly true. I used to think as I puddled about with dressings and Dakin through the hot, smoky, smelly afternoons in Outpatients, that it ought to say "All Cologne lives, dies, has its illegitimate and its legitimate brats, bleeds, smells and expectorates in the Central." (pp. 3–4)

Metaphor and simile, as in the passage above, often infuse the photographic, essentially visual, passages of Comfort's first five

novels. Also, the opening paragraph of *No Such Liberty* foreshadows
Comfort's emphasis in *The Power House, On This Side Nothing,* and
A Giant's Strength (especially in its opening paragraphs) upon
"height" in narration. In "The Angle of Narration," one of the chapters of *The Novel and Our Time,* Comfort writes that

One of the chief consequences of the cinematographic approach, . . . the
appreciation of the importance of *height* in securing effect, was already
evident in the work of Zola, Tolstoy, and Flaubert long before films were
invented. . . . In the recent novel the technical discoveries of Zola have been
extended in a remarkable degree, and for this extension I think the cinema is
largely responsible. (p. 38)

The essentially naturalistic method of description in Comfort's first
five novels is appropriate for Comfort whose scientific orientation
complements his role as a careful observer of external reality, interested in discerning cause-and-effect relationships. His scientific
orientation complements as well his abilities as a poet whose sensuous and particularized descriptions of external reality, as in his
elegies, work inductively: i.e., particularized descriptions, in both
his poetry and novels, are the means of adducing the general principles of human existence, of man as victim of external forces largely
beyond his control.

Comfort's view of society as fragmented, chaotic—a view which he
shares with the Apocalyptic writers—is, however, a more fundamental reason for his selection of realistic and naturalistic modes of
narration. Apocalyptic writers, such as Hendry and Treece, tried to
solve the problem of imposing meaning and order on external chaos,
in both their poetry and fiction, by the development of a highly
personal point of view: the artist both controls external disintegration, as well as escapes from it, by asserting his own sensibility and
private vision—what Hendry called private "myth"—against external disintegration. Comfort does this in his early poetry, but in his
novels orders flux and disintegration through objectivity—
realism—and the establishment of a narrative point of view. In *The
Novel and Our Time* he argues that "realism, the treatment of events
as they appear, is the method which appeals most directly in a period
when events are apocalyptic in character and scale" (p. 60), and that at

the present moment the literary interpretation of events is as much out of
control as the events themselves. . . . The problem of selection and coher-

ence . . . is soluble only by these two techniques, the dream-approach that obscures its reality, and the analytic approach that recognizes and isolates the common principle.

For me at any rate the solution which presents itself is to concentrate on the fixed-points, as one might look away from a fire to allow one's sight to settle down—the soldier in his pillbox watching Hitler's body burn, disliking the smoke, wondering if he will get a sanitary fatigue afterwards, and whether his wife has been killed. . . . (pp. 75–76)

In his *The Experimental Novel,* Zola, complaining of critics who accuse naturalistic writers of desiring solely to be photographers, notes that both scientific experiments and art involve selection and direction by the artist's or scientist's hypothesis, itself based on observation: "An experiment, even the most simple, is always based on an idea, itself born of an observation."[19] The logical as well as aesthetic unity of Comfort's novels has its basis in his vision of man as the victim of his environment. That naturalism provides an effective way of depicting victimized protagonists is Comfort's conclusion in *Art and Social Responsibility:* the "impulse in *Germinal*" lies in "the recognition of the irresponsibility of society," and the "essence of Naturalism," generally, "lies in its sense of victimhood now based upon scientific and no longer upon religious ideas . . ." (p. 47).

In *No Such Liberty* Breitz's victimization comes from irresponsible society, from institutionalized power. In *The Almond Tree,* more than in any other of his novels, Comfort focuses upon characters becoming aware of themselves as victims of a hostile or indifferent universe, victims, in other words, of death.

II   The Almond Tree

The Almond Tree (1942), Comfort's only historical novel, begins and ends in the farmhouse and vineyard in the Rhineland of the Tomasczewski family. Pyotr, a Polish emigrant, lives with his four grandchildren: Yelisaveta (the eldest, who with her German husband Karl manages the farm), Fyodor, Hilde, and Theresa. Serge, the fifth grandchild and heir, is away most of the time at Bonn, where he is a student of philosophy. After Pyotr's death, Yeli and Fyodor leave the farm. Fyodor becomes a student at a military academy, spends time at sea, and finally dies, from the yellow plague, on a lemon plantation in South America. Yeli goes to the household of Monsieur and Madame Roux in Paris to work as a companion for Madame Roux. After being sexually assaulted by Madame Roux, she lives for a while with Colin, her Parisian lover. She works in a convent after Colin's

departure as a soldier at the outbreak of the Great War, and finally
returns, after hearing of his death, to the Tomasczewski farm. Serge,
inducted as a German soldier, runs away in panic during an English
attack, is disabled by wounds inflicted during the attack, and finally
returns to the Tomasczewski farm with his wife, Lisa, who explains to
Yeli that she is "his wife," but "perhaps not in the ordinary sense of
the word."

The overall form of the novel, as Derek Stanford observes, may be
said to be circular:

> If, as E. M. Forster maintains, novels can be said to possess a shape, then this
> one of Comfort's is circular; with the almond tree as symbol at the centre—
> the one constant factor, to change the comparison, in an exhausting algebra of
> fate. . . . The image of the tree is like a pivot about which the lives of the
> characters revolve, and though existence may tarnish these people the
> symbol stands untouched in their minds; aloof, and lasting, to the end.[20]

The almond tree, Stanford correctly indicates, has different symbolic
implications for the various members of the Tomasczewski family,
but, according to Stanford, at the novel's conclusion is "a symbol of
now unattainable hope."[21] The narrator, possibly reflecting Yeli's
point of view, asserts at the novel's conclusion: "For this family the
tree meant only two things—the unattainable and the inevitable" (p.
203). The phrase "the unattainable and the inevitable" is used earlier
by Serge, and, as we shall see later, provides the novel with
philosophical dimensions and implications not accounted for by
Stanford or subsequent critics. That the eternally flourishing almond
tree is an ironic reminder of death and decay, impotence, Pyotr's
burdensome presence, and the vanity of existence is suggested by the
context in Ecclesiastes from which Comfort has taken his central
image. The epigraph of Book One reads: " 'The almond tree shall
flourish, and the grasshopper shall be a burden; and desire shall fail.'
Ecclesiastes." The passage in Ecclesiastes continues, "desire shall
fail; because man goeth to his everlasting home. . . . Vanity of
vanities, saith the Preacher; all is vanity" (12:5–8).

The Almond Tree has been reviewed by Edwin Muir and analyzed
by Derek Stanford and Robert Callahan. According to Muir, the
novel is "a work of original imagination," but "the whole course of the
story, which is intended to give a picture of the disintegration of life in
Europe between 1910 and 1920, is unconvincing."[22] Stanford sees
the novel essentially as "an illustrated thesis" of the theme that the

"pathos of life resides in recognizing the unattainable while helplessly committed, for all time, to the finite."[23] It is, in other words, a novel treating the Romantic anguish concerning the tragic, unbridgeable disparity between human aspirations and intractable reality. Stanford's criticism provides a good introduction to the novel. But by viewing it as a psychological study of the Romantic temperament, he is not impelled to provide an explanation of the genesis of such a temperament within the characters of the novel from the perspective of the historical period in which the events of the novel occur. Muir, also, fails to provide any explanation of the significance of its historical setting to the psychological types depicted within the novel, although Muir, correctly I believe, sees it as treating the "disintegration of life in Europe between 1910 and 1920." For Muir, fate (rather than psychological temperament) provides the motivation for action within the novel. He writes that if "one could believe in those diverse fates" which determine the various tragic conclusions of the lives of the characters then "the story would be very moving, but one cannot believe in them; one recognises them as mere illustrations of a general process which probably existed, but which Mr. Comfort has not grasped."[24]

Callahan's analysis provides an explanation of the disintegration of the lives of Comfort's characters from the perspective of their early psychological conditioning as members of the Tomasczewski household. *The Almond Tree*, Callahan writes, "observes outwardly self-sufficient individuals (in various domestic and social settings) who are actually disintegrating within as a consequence of irresolvable conflicts engendered during their upbringing."[25] Similarly, Stanford sees the novel as being in part a "study of maladjustment: of the members of a family to each other, and to the family as a whole. . . ." Theresa, Serge, Hilde, Yelisaveta and Fyodor are all "bent on escaping Pyotr's domination which warps and constricts their development," according to Stanford.[26] Such an interpretation is accurate as far as it goes. But it does not provide an adequate explanation of the novel's depiction of the psychological deterioration of two of its four chief protagonists, Serge and Yeli. Like other interpretations, moreover, it fails to provide an explanation of the relationship between the historical setting and the events within the novel. Callahan points out that "only in the most general sense are any of its situations drawn from and controlled by topical events and allusions," and concludes that chronology itself—which is emphasized by specifically dating each of six books on its title page—is the clearest evidence of an effort to clarify thematic intention by separating the intended effect of narrative from the distracting, inhibiting effects of contemporary events. It appears that Comfort decided to "purify" thematic intention by detaching the novel from both himself and the present, in order to simplify his diagnosis of the conflict between an individual and influences for anti-individualism, while enabling a reader to contemplate the social criticism involved rather than feel assaulted by it.[27]

Callahan's interpretation of Comfort's reason for dating the books of the novel is ingenious but farfetched. Comfort's indictments of contemporary manifestations of social irresponsibility—particularly in his depiction of Serge's disillusioning experiences in the Great War—are, and are presumably meant to be, relevant to events transpiring in Europe at the time that the novel is written. A satisfactory interpretation, however, must take into account that the novel directs the reader's attention to a particular historical period, partly by way of the explicit dating of its six books. It must also take into account that the novel generally does not link topical events with its depictions of the psychological development of its protagonists. Comfort's unfamiliarity with the period in question provides a partial explanation of such facts. But a view of the novel which explains psychological disintegration as largely the product of an overwhelming awareness of personal mortality will, I think, take such facts into account as well as explain them. The development of an awareness of death and attempts to escape from an awareness of death are causes in the novel of social disintegration. Since the awareness of death in the modern period is not the product of any public, topical event (with the exception of the Great War which functions as a watershed for the emergence of a pervasive consciousness of death in society in general), the novel's depiction of what Muir refers to as "the disintegration of life in Europe between 1910 and 1920" proceeds by way of explorations into the private psychological developments of its principle characters.

Furthermore, the subtitle of the novel, "A Legend," suggests that cultural development or decay will be represented not directly but emblematically. The subtitle implies that the novel has the force of what is normally referred to as a "myth" or "parable": i.e., a fictional account symbolically veiling a moral or psychological truth about a culture. Specifically, the novel treats the interlinking histories of the members of the Tomasczewski household, covering the period from

1910 through 1920. Through the memories of Pyotr Invanowicz it refers to events transpiring earlier. Mythically, the novel depicts the gradual emergence in the modern period of a widespread awareness of death and social disintegration, and foreshadows Comfort's explicit statements in *Art and Social Responsibility* concerning the historical setting in which such awarenesses have developed:

I rather doubt if ever in history there have been so many who realised the emotional fact of death. Megalopolitan civilisation is living under a death sentence. That has become a personal realisation over great areas of the world. . . . Slack water was at about 1900, and suddenly the face of social disintegration and personal death began to be seen by more and more people. The private knowledge of the Dostoievskys and Unamunos of the past was becoming general. . . . In some strange fashion the same knowledge, unconditioned by history, was growing up in innumerable childhoods—Dylan Thomas knew it early in life, long before the Spanish defeat. Art does not move always by sudden transition—Steiner's concept of the Zeitgeist is truer than it looks. The transition is a matter of relative numbers who reach a viewpoint together, independently. Artists reflect it now only because it is the general temper of the public. (p. 15)

The Almond Tree is Comfort's equivalent of Ramuz's *The Triumph of Death.*

Book One, entitled "A Patriarch 1910," is about Pyotr Invanowicz Tomasczewski, the grandfather of the family, and the effects which his patriarchal control of the family has upon its members. In the Tomasczewski household, authority is centralized, and made destructive, in the person of Pyotr. "He held the place together, a fixed pin through a bunch of lives and farm properties" (p. 12). Book One is also an exploration of senescence and the fear of death, comparable to Iris Murdoch's *Bruno's Dream.* Pyotr approximates that kind of thinking which Comfort characterizes above as "slack water." For Pyotr the earlier theological defenses against death no longer apply, but he resists admitting into consciousness the fact of death as personal extinction. In the early parts of the novel he knows intellectually that he probably has not long to live. But he usually avoids thinking about death, or else uses the fact that he will probably die in the near future in order to manipulate those around him. A stroke and his subsequent convalescence cause him to reflect more seriously upon death, but he attempts to interpret death in such a way that he will not have to face death as annihilation.

Shortly before Pyotr dies he imagines that death may actually involve some sort of victory over time and personal disintegration. His deathbed meditations concerning his metamorphosis into the security and permanence of the objective world recall the ending of Read's *The Green Child* and provide a criticism, but probably not an actual parody, of the kind of acquiescence in death which Read portrays in *The Green Child* and advocates in other works: Olivero in part three of Read's novel delights in the thought of the objectivity of death and is fortunate enough to have his desires realized by being petrified. Pyotr consoles himself with the thought that dying "would be like climbing among the leaves" of the almond tree (p. 60), and climbing to the center of the almond tree would be to "sit like a spider, static in a drop of resin" (p. 59). "Perhaps," he muses, death "was just growing static like a stone. The idea appealed to his streak of conservatism, and he chuckled. Anyhow, it was not terrible" (p. 60).

As Pyotr had believed, his own death is not terrible, not terrible in his own understanding, and involves, in the moments before he dies, a belief that his existence has become static, preserved from the ravages of time. The only extended death scene in Comfort's works, Comfort's description of Pyotr's last dying moments provides an impressive conclusion to the first book of *The Almond Tree*. (Derek Stanford refers to this section of the novel as "a few pages of pure sensuous beauty. . . ."[28]) At the beginning of chapter five of Book One Pyotr is partially paralyzed from the effects of the stroke brought on by Otto's drunken behavior, but he has "begun to talk a little more distinctly" (p. 57). He spends time remembering that past, but with growing confusion. A final sleepiness completes the deadening of the rational, conceptual aspects of his mind, already confused by senility and the effects of the stroke; and his imagination takes over, fusing and confusing his very earliest memories with more recent memories:

In Pyotr's mind the cradle with the apple faces tipped to and fro, in the sun which fell through the white posts of the farm balcony at Lowicz, and bees dangled shimmering at the end of an unwinding string over his face. He crinkled up his small pink face at the sunlight and somebody covered him with a green cloth, all the little holes in it shining like stars. It was like being under the sea. . . . Pyotr's mother hummed to him. Then the green cloth was taken away and his mother took him up, dazzled, and he buried his face. He remembered how warm and smooth her breast was, and how it shaded his face as he nuzzled into it. She held his two feet in her hand as he drank, and he curled his toes with pleasure. He could never focus her face clearly, for his sight did not go far enough. But it was mottled with the finger shadows of the tree. He was put back in the impression his head made on the cradle pillow. . . . He screwed up his face and slept. Always like this. The green cloth and the stars, just out of his reach: the cradle. It would never change, and he did not care for to-morrow. It would be time soon for another warm drink. His middle was round and comfortable. He slept, dreaming about the hard feel of the table when they laid him on it after his bath.

And he was still under the green cloth when he awoke again. There were voices all around him. His mother's voice, Marya's, Dimitri's. He lay in his cradle, looking forward outside the courtyard he couldn't see, hearing his wife speaking, knowing she was looking down on him, with his mother. And Dimitri—or was it his father? It must be his father, because Dimitri was not born. Marya and his mother talking together. Maria, causa laetitiae nostrae. . . . The sun rippled over his cloth. He could hear the words they said plainly, but he was too young to understand them.

"He doesn't know us," whispered Theresa. "Yeli, my dear—speak to him."

"Grandfather!" . . .

But he did not care. The sun was on him, and he was fed and warm.

But out of all those faces, who was the dark, sloe-eyed girl with the black plaits wound round her head? Was it Marya? He couldn't remember if it was she or not.

"He's going," said Dr. Leibnitz.

"Marya," said Pyotr. "Marya."

Yelisaveta took his hand. "Not Marya. Yeli."

The leaves flicker a little all around him. The stars began to go out. Not Marya. Yeli. Or Helena? No, she was fair-haired. Not Marya. . . .

The cloth vanished, and he was looking up at his mother, but her face was too far off for him to see it clearly. He burrowed for her breast, but he couldn't find it, and whimpered. Yeli smoothed his forehead. He was tired and pettish at not being fed. But he was still in his cradle. He could always go to sleep. He burrowed into the pillow, and the cloth was laid over him. Always like this. He dropped off to sleep again.

Dr. Leibnitz nodded, and Yeli drew the counterpane over Pyotr's face. (pp. 60–63)

Both Pyotr's impending death and the death scene described above deeply affect the members of his family—especially Fyodor. Pyotr's physical and mental disintegration is repeatedly emphasized in Book One, and his presence functions as a constant reminder to all of his household of the inescapability of death and decay. On the other hand, his patriarchal domination of his household in the name of the unquestioned values of the past is a reminder by contrast of the threat of social disintegration which faces modern society. The two problems are related and given conscious expression in the experiences of Serge and Yeli.

In trying to explain to Lisa why he is unable to write his thesis in philosophy, Serge notes that when he locks the door to his room in order to write he does "Nothing," for the certainty of death and the absence of certainty in the realm of moral values pale everything else. He has found only "two certainties," he explains to Lisa: the "inevitable and the unattainable." Death, essentially, is the inevitable, and "knowing what to do next and why to do it" is the "unattainable" (p. 155). Later, in language reminiscent of the nihilistic conclusions reached by Ivan after reciting the legend of the Grand Inquisitor in *The Brothers Karamazov*, Serge talks to Yeli about his desertion from the army:

"It wasn't running away that spoiled me. It was knowing that you could run away and it didn't matter. I've found out what I wanted to know. It doesn't matter what one does. Anything is as good as anything else. I was always afraid I should find that out, but I hoped my mind would not let me believe it. . . ."

"Serge, what is going to happen when other people find out? It's no good pretending. The first time I knew was when I saw somebody die, and realized that they were done with, and no more talking. But what will happen if everyone finds out?"

"That's why I daren't go on writing. Everyone will find out. And then hell will break loose." (p. 205)

The loss of absolute values, leading to social disintegration, and the realization of personal death, are linked in the passage above. The disappearance of absolute ethical standards is understood by Serge and Yeli as being partly the consequence of the realization that there are no lasting values because human beings do not last, because the values that men believe in are lost with them when they die. Such a conclusion is intimated earlier in Serge's Christmas dinner conversation with Dr. Leibnitz (a friend of the family whose enthusiasm for life suggests that for Dr. Leibnitz, as for the philosopher Leibnitz, this is the best of all possible worlds). In response to Dr. Leibnitz's questions concerning his thesis, Serge observes: "I'm beginning to think that a criminal is only somebody who believes he's not immortal after all . . ." (p. 52). Inasmuch as God—who in the Western tradition has provided the guarantee of both individual immortality and the existence of absolute values—no longer plays a part in Serge's and Yeli's thinking or in the modern consciousness with which they are concerned, it is perhaps of some significance that Serge's dissertation was to be on Nietzsche (p. 51). In *Joyful Wisdom* Nietzsche's notorious madman is a harbinger for modern thought of the knowledge that God is dead.

Fyodor, by way of contrast, never achieves Serge's and Yeli's level of awareness. But Fyodor's awareness of meaninglessness and death surpasses that of Pyotr and may be understood as symbolizing or suggesting a transitional phase in the development of modern consciousness. The sea represents to Fyodor freedom from power-oriented individuals and institutions (as it does to the narrator of *The Silver River*) and from an awareness of death. However, his perception of the death of the engineer breaks his Edenic existence at sea, and is a revelation of the horror and senselessness of death as personal annihilation, a more profound comprehension of death than Pyotr's: "If anybody had told him he was about to see this, he would have fainted. But now there was only one picture, that of the red end of a bone, which he wished to uproot from his mind. To do so he shut his eyes again, and thought of the tree. This was the second death he had seen, unlike the death of Pyotr in his bed thinking he was a baby. Somebody had gone on to that deck expecting to come up again and hadn't. He wondered where the engineer was, and knew at once that he was nowhere" (pp. 147–48). Such insights are largely obscured by Fyodor's subsequent idyllic existence on a South American plantation. But his own death is as meaningless as the death of the engineer. Whereas Serge realizes intellectually the purposeless hostility of nature, Fyodor experiences it; he dies from the plague and is buried with the other plague deaths "not in the ground, but in the wall outside Iquique, . . . number 1,795, and not a tree in sight" (p. 188).

Yeli is associated in Fyodor's mind with a sexuality of a vague, undifferentiated—i.e., adolescent—sort. His incestuous yearnings for his sister are fused with his vaguely homosexual desires for a hermaphroditic child—the product of his imagination—which, like the almond tree, represents for Fyodor an escape from a universe dominated by time and death. Fyodor's perverted fantasies are in part the product of his upbringing in the repressive environment of the Tomasczewski household and his subsequent experiences in a military academy which fosters masturbation but suppresses other forms of sexual expression. Furthermore, such perversions are also, more generally, reactions on Fyodor's part to a professedly Christian and repressive society which has come to emphasize what Comfort in

Sex in Society refers to as the "sadistic topics of Christian iconography," but which impedes any realistic acceptance of death. Unlike Fyodor, Yeli has some ability to deal with such a society without escaping from it. While temporarily living in a convent, Yeli is "defiantly happy" in the thought that "in this spiritually aseptic place, she was the only woman bar the cleaners who wasn't a virgin" (p. 192). She realizes as well that authoritarian behavior and thinking are the means of obscuring or avoiding a confrontation with death, as well as life. Consequently, she is able to observe that the members of the convent were "so certain of themselves, grinning at death like a child smiles at the gun that is going to shoot it—not understanding" (p. 191).

Yeli's experiences in the home in Paris of Monsieur and Madame Roux introduce her to sexual perversions more serious, because more destructive, than those of Fyodor. Ultimately Madame Roux attempts a lesbian rape upon Yeli, but her embroidery suggests the combination in her personality of lesbian and sadomasochistic tendencies. The "pink naked body" of St. Catherine is "sprawled across" her embroidery, and Yeli watches Madame Roux "sticking in her needle with a very quiet little smile" (p. 74). Yeli subsequently sees Madame "pricking away at St. Catherine's wounds, stroking her knee up and down" in masturbatory reverie (p. 81). Her sublimation of sexual energy into superficially nonsexual activity and expression is of an obsessional character, and presumably functions as a means of excluding from consciousness the earlier "unpleasantness" in which she was involved (p. 72). The specifically religious nature of her obsession may be accounted for as a kind of reaction formation, as defined by Freud.

Unlike all of Comfort's other novels, *The Almond Tree* provides the reader with no exemplary character who is able to perceive the facts of personal annihilation and social disintegration without being destroyed by such a perception. Serge retreats to the Tomasczewski farm a defeated man, physically debilitated, and sexually, as well as spiritually, impotent. Yeli is ultimately terrified by her "vision of a world filled with millions of desperate people, seeing their end, and knowing that there was nowhere to go and no rules to obey" (p. 206). In *No Such Liberty* such awareness is inhibited by the narrator's sanguine assumption that traditional values are still applicable. In *The Power House* and Comfort's subsequent novels his protagonists know, or discover, that a realistic acceptance of personal mortality need not be debilitating and that values are not arbitrarily chosen.

In its circular structure, its polyphonic interweaving of the narrative and imagery of its six books, and its symbolic and mythic texture, *The Almond Tree* is the most poetic and most symphonic of all of Comfort's novels. Images recur and gather meaning as the narrative proceeds, as in Book Three, in which Fyodor's hazy meditations, recalling Pyotr's confused awareness of being rocked in a cradle under a green cloth as he lies dying, have ominous implications: "The captain had undone his belt and his cigar came over in waves, its smoke becoming suddenly luminous in the interstices of the leaves. Fyodor had an irresistible feeling, as the shadows swung, that he was being rocked in a cradle, under a green cloth, but why he should feel so he did not know" (p. 135). Comfort's next novel, *The Power House*, returns to, and improves upon, the naturalistic, essentially unambiguous mode of narration employed in *No Such Liberty*. But in its employment of an omniscient narrator and its treatment of the disintegration of a culture, in a manner more epic than symphonic in character, *The Power House* extends the narrative technique and subject matter of *The Almond Tree*.

III   The Power House

The Power House (1944) begins in an industrial town in France before the outbreak of World War II. Fougueux, the principal character of Book One, and Loubain are mechanics in the power house of a textile factory owned by M. Duneulin. After Loubain murders a young woman, Arsule, he and Fougueux escape by truck at the conclusion of Book One, and reappear as soldiers in Book Two in a seaside military unit which includes two lieutenants, Vernier and Vatlin. Vernier, "a tall anxious man with a taste for literature and a dislike of decision," is the principle character of Book Two. Vatlin, who feigns sickness at the conclusion of Book Two in order to avoid being moved to the front, is a catalyst in Vernier's gradual awakening to the psychopathological character of violence, war, and society generally. Book Three is largely about the disillusioning experiences of Vernier, Loubain, and Fougueux in battle and disorderly retreat from the victorious German army. Book Four depicts the experiences of Vernier, Vatlin, Loubain, and Fougueux in occupied Paris, introduces the four to Ritter, a German officer, and recounts conspiratorial acts which lead to the deaths of Vatlin and Loubain. In the fifth and final book, Fougueux and Vernier, now prisoners, are put to work in Duneulin's factory, now under German control but managed with Duneulin's cooperation. Vernier befriends Claus, a rebellious eccentric who also serves as a catalyst in Vernier's intellectual and moral development. Inasmuch as the novel begins and ends, essentially, in the town of Book One, its shape parallels that of *The Almond Tree*, or, as Callahan observes, is circular ("comes full circle in its last book"). [29]

The Power House elicited a fair amount of attention from reviewers. Henry Reed in the *New Statesman and Nation* argued that the "people and scenes" of the novel were "merely a miscellany of conventional literary matter, fashionable things to put inside a sophisticated book." [30] Dan S. Norton in the *New York Times Book Review* saw the novel as "an interesting failure" and found the characters and actions of the work to be improbable. [31] In a review for the *Chicago Sun Book Week* André Maurois noted that Fougueux and Loubain appear as "real workmen of Northern France" and that "the author knows very well the little world he is writing about." Maurois went on to conclude that *The Power House* was "not perhaps a great book," yet it was "the book of a man who can write great books because he has both the lyrical intensity and the power to create." [32]

John Farrar in the *Saturday Review of Literature* went further than Maurois by praising Comfort as "an author of remarkable talent, possibly of genius." Farrar saw *The Power House* as "certainly among the few challenging books of fiction produced by a young man in these war years." [33] Marjorie Farber in the *New Republic* similarly found Comfort to be an "extraordinarily talented young British artist," and *The Power House* to be a "brilliant novel." [34] Diana Trilling, in a review for *The Nation*, found the novel to be among those "too dull or opaque to finish," and, consequently, did not finish it:

Because of its author's place among the younger British intellectuals, "The Power House" claimed my attention. It was not able to engage it. I read the first two dozen pages three times without having any notion of what I was reading; then I made several firm attempts to break into the story at a later point of its development, each time without success. [35]

In an enthusiastic review written for *The Spectator*, Kate O'Brien observed that the

greatness of Mr. Comfort's book is that in it he has truly exposed the bleak and broken hearts of millions of his fellowmen; if he and a few others of his generation can see so unblinkingly the pass to which humanity has brought itself, perhaps there is hope. . . . The book . . . has a moral, and presents it bravely. It is a very fine, true novel. May it be read as it deserves to be! [36]

Despite the diversity of opinion concerning its artistic merits, reviews of the novel, as well as criticism, have been generally sensible and perceptive.

Its style has attracted the attention of a number of its critics. Norton thought that although the novel was "full of objective details and subjective impressions," its effect was "usually thin and dream-like. . . ." O'Brien saw a plausible explanation for Comfort's style in its relationship to the French literary tradition, noting that the "method of narration—deriving much more from French than from English tradition—is monotone and somewhat elliptical. . . ." *The Power House* is not a novel of characters in the traditional sense, and in its often dreamlike presentation of the surface of things it bears a superficial resemblance to the novels of Alain Robbe-Grillet.

In its grim, detailed depictions of a social and physical environment which oppresses and largely determines the responses of its characters, particularly in Book One, *The Power House* is the most thoroughly naturalistic of Comfort's novels. But no rigid determinism is at work. The realm of rigid necessity in the novel is the realm of mindless acquiescence in corporate psychopathology. The general process of character development, in this respect, is that of characters whose ideas and behavior are the product of the environment in which they subsist becoming characters who are related to their physical and social environment by virtue of reacting against it. Vernier, in particular, develops the kind of anarchist philosophy which works against his being manipulated by environment, even while he is a political prisoner.

The dominant symbols of the novel are the power house and the slaughterhouse at which Fougueux works, in sequence, in Book One. As much is suggested by Farrar's astute comment that Comfort's "intention is definite and noble. He tells us the story of his power house, of his slaughter house; of France at war and in occupation, of labor struggle and sabotage, of every noble intention turned to dust, of the perversion, insanity, and ruin of war and revolution." The power house in particular is an ambiguous symbol and both it and the slaughterhouse have meanings which are complementary and inter-related. However, simply stated, the power house and the slaughterhouse symbolize power and death, the dominant motifs, I believe, of the novel.

Slaughterhouse symbolism appears elsewhere in Comfort's works, and it has in *The Power House* similar implications. The representation in the opening chapter of the factory workers returning home, herded together like sheep, implies the kind of unprotesting com-

pliance to an exploitative social and economic system that is implied
by Comfort's description in *The Silver River* of a meat canning factory
representing a society into which "holocausts of human beings . . .
march daily, emerging as canned personalities, canned minds, recep-
tacles for chemically sterile ideas, approved for safe circulation by the
powers that be" (pp. 70–71). In *The Power House* Fougueux, walking
home from the textile factory, becomes lost in a crowd of workers:

> The invisible crowd was closing in, coughing, and the patter of their feet on
> the clinker changed to the sound of sheep trotting and shuffling over the
> cobbles. There were bleating sneezes and words all round. He was sur-
> rounded by millions of invisible sheep. . . .
> He thought he saw Loubain ahead, knowing him by his height and his
> shock of hair, and yelled after him, but he did not turn. The crowd was filing
> together, queueing like sheep to be dipped, waiting the turn to file over the
> narrow catwalk of the sluice gates on the middle canal. . . . (pp. 10–11)

Such imagery anticipates and complicates the later description of the
slaughterhouse in which Fougueux is temporarily employed, and this
latter and literal slaughterhouse in turn symbolically foreshadows
Comfort's depictions of the butchery of men like cattle during the
war.

  Doheny correctly views the title of the novel as referring to "both
the actual power house and the world as a whole," and the "power
house metaphor as the main unifying element in the novel. . . ."[37]
Less generally, the power house is a symbol for a number of interrelated forms of power. The centralized power of capitalistic industrialism is represented in Book One by the textile factory and its
power house. Capitalism is depicted as producing according to profit
rather than need and finding in militarism a natural ally, suggested in
part by the fact that the workers are forced to wear carpet slippers,
with cardboard soles, instead of shoes as the factories turn to the
production of war materials. As in Zola's *Germinal*, capitalism and
industrialism, by forcing workers into crowded living quarters in
proximity of the factory or mine, are responsible for making privacy
impossible. And it is "lack of privacy," as Callahan observes,[38] or "the
overcrowded living in an economically depressed area," as Doheny
observes,[39] which is one of the causes of Fougueux's impotency.

  The novel in a number of ways anticipates the vision of society in
Comfort's *Barbarism and Sexual Freedom* in which "leisure, privacy,
security, community and responsibility," the "essential physical

conditions for sexual normality," are denied by a society which "combines unparalleled technical equipment with extreme personal insecurity and congestion with loneliness" (p. 7). The scene at the beginning of the novel of the blinding fog in which shadowy figures grope and jostle each other symbolizes, among other things, such a paradoxical combination of congestion with loneliness. More generally, it is reminiscent of similar nightmarish visions of urbanized existence in Dickens, Joyce, Eliot, and Sartre.

In later sections the power house also functions as a symbol of military power. At the novel's conclusion Duneulin's textile factory and power house are surrounded by a city leveled by Allied air raids and have become German property, worked by Allied prisoners. *La Virginie* (the machine of the power house) is finally destroyed by rioting prisoners who do not want to be moved east into Germany or Poland. But the implications of their destruction reach further, suggesting the frustrated opposition of the weak and the disobedient against entrenched, dehumanizing power in all its variegated forms.

But violence is not the alternative to entrenched power in the novel, and the time for nonviolent expropriation of factories by workers has not yet arrived. In the allegorical world of *Cities of the Plain* the anarcho-syndicalist vision of the revolutionary general strike may be realized. In the comparatively realistic world of the novel the insurrection of the workers at the power house, while suggesting something about the necessity of the revolutionary attitude, accomplishes nothing of practical value and results in a number of deaths.

Individual or conspiratorial acts of terrorism (the sort of terrorism that still defines anarchism in the popular mind) are also counteractive. Vernier and Fougueux become part of a conspiracy to dynamite a trail filled with German troops, but blow up a passenger train full of farmers and women by mistake. Vernier, who has engaged in the conspiracy in order to avenge the death of the anarchist Vatlin, concludes, " 'I think Vatlin would have had the sense not to do that. Vatlin realized that when one attempts to take personal action it miscarries. You can't hit history—an innocent person always comes between' " (p. 379). Claus makes essentially the same observation concerning the unproductiveness of opposing violence with violence (or power with power) at the conclusion of the novel (p. 460) and envisions the final victory of the weak (p. 459).

As in *The Triumph of Death* submersion of individuality within the collective is a means of gaining the illusion that one has escaped from

death, contingency, and finitude. But the collective is not explicitly
the state. The German officer Ritter, according to the narrator, had
not "been able to realize how much, in his youth, his own battle with
the fear of death had cost him in personal and mental independence"
(p. 348). The state does not die, or at least will not disintegrate in the
foreseeable future, and hence it offers the hope of vicarious immortality. When Ritter believes that he will have to turn Vernier over to the
German authorities for murder and treason, Vernier tells Ritter:
" 'No. I don't want to be shot. I'm as terrified of death as you are. You
teach yourself to be callous with your own life and with other people's
and you work up a belief that the State is immortal. I can see through
that' " (p. 380). When Ritter responds by charging, "you believe
nothing," Vernier observes that living without "myths" means facing
"up to the fact that you die" (p. 380).

Earlier, Vatlin, drunk, muses to Ritter, Vernier, and Fougueux on
the possibility of establishing a priesthood that would be aware that
life ends in extinction, but would teach the masses to believe in
immortality in order to keep them happy. (Such a possibility is
explored in Unamuno's *Saint Emmanuel the Good, Martyr* to which
Comfort may be indebted.) As in *The Almond Tree* common morality
depends upon keeping the masses in ignorance of the fact of personal
annihilation:

> I often think we want a priesthood, a sort of secret society . . . and limited to
> twelve members; and they teach doctrines of goodness and immortality and
> the rest of it to the public. And of course, the mystery which the twelve keep
> to themselves is simply that one dies. It doesn't do to let that out—the twelve
> keep a censorship on the Sadducees . . . because decent behavior depends
> on the public not discovering that our idea of purpose is bogus. . . .
>
> It would appeal to my ideas of self-sacrifice to be one of the twelve—talking
> what I knew was bilge to keep the rest of mankind happy. I should be a sort of
> moral anesthetist—I should almost be being crucified. (pp. 320–21)

But society has already found out, Vatlin goes on to conclude.
Employing an analogy used elsewhere in Comfort's fiction, he describes modern Europeans in war attempting en masse to suppress,
through despairing, purposeless, and self-destructive activity, the
knowledge of death: "In this bloody Europe we're just so many
lemming, swimming out to sea, and all cheering like bloody hell to
see which sinks first" (p. 322).

Such irrational self-destructiveness is prima facie evidence within
the world of the novel for the madness of collective behavior.

Comfort's depictions of war in Books Two and Three illustrate that it is not anarchists, such as Vatlin, who are the purveyors of madness, disorder, and chaos, but the state itself. The primary symbol of anarchy (defined simply as social chaos) in the novel is the confused and disorganized battle in which Vernier engages and the subsequent chaotic retreat of Vernier and his men in Book Three. The mental hospital at which they momentarily stop for food while retreating, and immediately after passing soldiers who "yelled like lunatics" (p. 281), ironically underscores the psychopathology of society at war.

The Power House, as several of its critics have observed, depicts human existence which has become mechanized. For example, Farber intimates the Kafkaesque suggestiveness of Comfort's images of mechanized human beings, and sees in them a technique to suggest dissociated thinking. Objections raised by Farrar and Reed to the novel's particularized descriptions and its profusion of similes are partially answered by the realization that a number of such descriptions and figures of speech have the thematic function of intimating the mechanization of life within the urban environment of Book One. People rumble "like machinery" (p. 48), Fougueux's aunt has a neck which troubles her by throbbing "like an engine" (p. 44), Jeanlin laughs to herself "like a part of a machine drowning, like *La Virginie*" (p. 133), Fougueux dreams of Melusine "weaning power into him, slowly, like the starting of a machine from dead center" (p. 115). The reader is informed that Chardonne had been "able to erect a new fantasy of himself as the efficient machine" (p. 190), mechanical cranes are compared to cranes as birds (p. 56), and so forth.

The traditional Romantic and anarchist distinction between the organic and the mechanic is at work in Comfort's descriptions, a distinction which is carried over into neo-Romantic literature. Godwin was concerned about authoritarian institutions reducing "the exertions of a human being to the level of a piece of mechanism . . . alleviated by no genuine passion."[40] "The mass of men serve the state," Thoreau declared, ". . . not as men mainly, but as machines, with their bodies."[41] In Read's *The Parliament of Women*, Helena argues that the "worst treachery is to deny the impulses of the heart," and Anna argues that it is necessary to "impose a pattern on life." The freedom of the heart that Helena desires includes a freedom from oppressive political organizations, and the pattern imposed on life which Anna advocates is a pattern of "rank," of "knights and knight's ladies," and of "lawful ways."[42]

Similarly, in *The Power House* the mechanization of life is not to be accounted for simply on the basis of the traditional Romantic criticism of bourgeois society as being destructive of the imagination, art, or the harmonious unification of unconscious and conscious elements of the personality, although such aesthetic and psychological elements are involved. *The Power House*, like *The Parliament of Women* as well as part two of *The Green Child,* depicts a society in which the mechanical has usurped the organic, and the mechanization of life is fundamentally the product of power-orientation within society.

Callahan indicates Comfort's indebtedness to the opposition in Apocalyptic thought between "individual myth" and the mechanized modes of existence engendered by conformity to "social myth," as defined by Hendry: "Finding himself in a world of realized desire, city and garden, which is nevertheless demonic, the Apocalyptic writer welcomed the fact, Hendry argued, that 'the machine age' in which we live, with its terrifying objectivity, has revived the myth as a mode of release. . . ."[43] At the conclusion of his chapter on *The Almond Tree,* Callahan remarks that "Comfort's fiction shows that man can work at his 'individual myth' in spite of allegedly terminal barbarism. . . ."[44]

The Apocalyptic writers did not continue to adhere to their original philosophical premises. Comfort's attitudes towards myth and mechanization are closer to those developed by Fraser than to those of Treece. In "A Letter to Henry Treece" (included in *Transformation Four*), Fraser reaffirms his opposition to "the ideal of a mechanical order," but expresses his increasing disillusionment with the notion of individual myth (i.e., "the danger of an acceptance, too uncritical, of one's own myths").[45] Treece answers Fraser's letter by explaining his own ability to retain his independence in the "machine" of the R.A.F., and observing that Fraser and his "comrades *en masse*" are "suffering from a persecution mania." Treece informs Fraser,

The man who lacks a goal is already half-lost. Conversely, the man who has forced for himself some purpose, some goal, provided it be a Christian purpose and goal, is proof against corruption. For is not corruption only another way of compensating for one's lack of faith in one's self and one's fellows; is it not only a substitute for happiness and completeness?

Lack of faith, corruption, an uneasy conscience, fear of the machine, fear of one's fellows, fear of love. . . . All these I see as a contemporary disease. You confess, whether you like it or not, that you suffer from some of these troubles, and I am smugly glad that at the moment I don't.[46]

In contrast, Comfort's works express a continuing antipathy towards hierarchically structured, authoritarian institutions and the attendant mechanization of human existence. The fundamental psychological and moral antithesis in Comfort's novels, moreover, is not that of "individual myth" against "social myth" per se, but individual, demythologized reason against irrational patterns of belief—held privately or publicly—and authority.

Farrar correctly observes that in *The Power House* the "theme of physical and mental impotence is a challenging one," and that Fougueux's sexual impotence in Book One and Vernier's intellectual impotence in later books "are both parallel and opposed in this complicated symbolism." Where the identification of persons with machines and machines with persons is given a specifically sexual significance, Fougueux's sexual impotence usually is the subject. While he tends *La Virginie* the machine's moving "cluster of rods" cause "ecstatic little cries" which rise to a "climax" and remind Fougueux of his sister making little cries as she makes love to Chaumette (pp. 37–38). Such sounds from the machine also cause Fougueux to remember a setting suggesting sexual impotence, the deserted gun emplacements of Fort Risban, in which he first discovered in the contempt of a light-haired Walloon girl his sexual impotence (p. 38). He thinks of the "warm body of the machine" as he remembers the girl's contempt, and then sees Loubain drop "golden oil into the snuffbox oilers" (p. 390).

The orgastic significance of "golden oil" is exploited again when Fougueux is "so consumed with jealousy" at seeing one of the other workers—the "Monkey"—"running his eyes over" the machine "from one end to another, as if she were naked," that Fougueux can "hardly drop the gold thread of oil straight into the oilers" (p. 62). Towards Melusine, later, he is also sexually attracted, but still impotent. The narrator informs us that "there were times when he confused her, quite fully and quite unintentionally, with *La Virginie*, the two images of her body and of the intricacies of the machine superimposing themselves on each other" (p. 45).

Fougueux's sexual impotence is symbolic of a society in which individuals generally have lost the capacity to relate to each other as persons and relate to each other as objects. Somewhat like that of Eliot's Fisher King and of Serge in *The Almond Tree*, his sexual impotence is also symbolic of contemporary sterility, meaninglessness and emptiness. The description of the huge tower of the textile factory—an "enormous phallus racing across the clouds"—that

Fougueux attempts to climb (p. 75 ff.) and of the barren yard in back
of his house in which Fougueux, attempting to cultivate something,
discovers that nothing grows (pp. 17 and 61) help to symbolize the
emptiness and powerlessness of Fougueux's existence and of French
society.

Comfort's depiction of sexual impotence in *The Power House*
anticipates his view in *Barbarism and Sexual Freedom* that the "first
attribute of barbarism is impotence, in every sense of the word" (p.
10). His depictions of sadism and masochism in the characters of
Loubain, Arsule, and Fougueux suggest the same sort of conclusion
concerning the cause-and-effect relationship between cultural and
individual pathology that is explicitly made by Comfort in *Barbarism
and Sexual Freedom* when he argues that sadism and masochism are
"liable to become" necessary attributes of "citizenship under barbarism. . ." (p. 11).

Conventional attitudes towards sexual behavior, in the light of
Comfort's libertarian views, should not be applied by the reader to
the sexual behavior of characters within the novel. For example,
Fougueux's tying of Melusine's hands with his neck-cloth in order to
elicit sexual response (p. 125)—despite its unconventional and seemingly perverse character—is not, in itself, psychopathological; for its
effects are not destructive to the interests or well-being of the parties
involved (although Fougueux is chagrined at his lack of success.)

Fougueux's attitude towards Arsule, who he views as merely a
woman "it would be a pleasure to hurt" (p. 84), and Loubain's similar
attitude towards Arsule are, by contrast, fundamentally pathological.
When Loubain ties Arsule's hands with a cord off her dressing gown
upon her request, Arsule's masochistic behavior elicits from Loubain
a brutal and fatally sadistic response. Before fleeing from the police,
Loubain explains to Fougueux the circumstances surrounding Arsule's death:

"I wanted her, boy, you know that. But she wanted me to kill her, always. She
went after you and Michel because she thought I wasn't strong enough. I took
her but she fought me—she kept yelling, 'Hurt me, hurt me.' I was scared,
but she wouldn't let go. She got the cord off her dressing gown and made me
tie her with it. She was mad, I tell you. Then I couldn't stop holding her, and
suddenly she was dead." (p. 131).

Superficially, the situation recalls Comfort's observation in *Sex in
Society*—repeated later, in effect, in *The Joy of Sex*—that "the plea-

sure which a few people derive from partial strangulation may easily lead to their own death and a murder charge against their partner. . ." (p. 25). But the implications of Arsule's death are more serious. Not only is power-oriented society within the world of the novel productive of sadistic and masochistic behavior, but it is conjointly directed towards, and destructively preoccupied with, death. Arsule is obsessed with, as well as sexually excited by, violence and death. When Fougueux is working at the slaughterhouse, he notices her among the children who have come to watch the slaughter:

Then at the end he suddenly saw Arsule. She was standing on a metal oil drum, nearest to the engines. . . . Her eyes were as round and as glased as those of the cattle, and her nostrils went in and out as she breathed. Her face was utterly fixed on the killing, on the moving arms of the men. She gasped visibly between her lips. (p. 102)

Comfort's depiction of Arsule's sadomasochistic personality owes something, but not much, to Freud's later views concerning masochism and sadism as manifestations of a self-destructive impulse in human nature (the proverbial Freudian "death instinct"). But it is unlikely that Arsule's behavior can be accounted for as simply the consequence of a self-destructive impulse, despite the belief of Loubain and the comment of a sympathetic narrator—reflecting, at this point in the narrative, Fougueux's point of view—that she wishes to be murdered (pp. 130–31). Rather, her impulse towards self-destructiveness is a manifestation of the sort of "ambivalent attempt at once to court and reject suffering" which Comfort in *Art and Social Responsibility* links with the appearance of "sadomasochist traits in the public at large," and which ultimately represents the "exorcism of Death" (p. 62).

But sadomasochistic behavior in the novel is also a means of escaping from isolation (the fear of death, for Comfort, being "probably at root the fear of isolation"[47]) and powerlessness. And in this sense Comfort's treatment of Arsule's and Loubain's sadomasochistic behavior basically parallels Erich Fromm's argument in *The Fear of Freedom* that it is not ultimately pain and self-destruction which the sadomasochistic personality desires, but an escape from intolerable feelings of personal powerlessness and isolation. In this sense, also, the explicitly sexual perversions of Book One anticipate Comfort's subsequent treatment of sadomasochistic tendencies disconnected from their explicitly erotic components. Such tendencies express themselves in the willingness of men at war to escape from individual powerlessness and isolation by submitting blindly to the institutionalized power of the military and the state or by exercising power over others within the framework of such institutions.

Sadistic impulses also manifest themselves, disconnected from their explicitly erotic components, as simple violence and destructiveness: in particular, the sexually sadistic behavior of Loubain in Book One anticipates Comfort's subsequent descriptions of the violence and destructiveness of war. That war is an especially appropriate vehicle for the expression of sexually sadistic impulses is suggested by Loubain's patriotic and militaristic enthusiasm when Vernier, his commanding officer, realistically perceives that the French forces have been beaten (p. 279).

In his first three novels Comfort may be considered a philosophical novelist whose characters are not essentially concerned with analyzing or elaborating upon the theories of others, but who discover personal redemption through the development of reason and a sense of moral responsibility. Like the characters of Thomas Hardy, Comfort's are victimized by a hostile environment: social institutions irresponsive to human needs and an indifferent universe. *The Almond Tree* is Comfort's first and last experiment in a mythical and musical, or poetic, mode of creation, somewhat analogous to that of Joyce or Virginia Woolf. The naturalistic, photographic techniques employed in *No Such Liberty* and *The Power House* are employed also in Comfort's subsequent novels. But in none of his later novels does he focus so predominantly as he does in *The Power House* on an exhaustive (and for some readers, apparently exhausting) analysis of the physical environments in which his characters subsist.

CHAPTER 3

Later Novels

A S a naturalist Comfort might be expected to carefully examine not
only the social environment in which his characters exist, but
hereditary tendencies and early experiences within the family as
well. In none of his novels, except *The Almond Tree*, is this the case,
and only in *The Power House* does he give much attention to the
influences which family life—not early experiences—exerts on
character formation. The focus of his fiction is upon an analysis of
asocial collectives based on power and upon the overwhelming
impact which such collectives have upon the psychological development of his protagonists. It is partly in this light that it is dramatically
appropriate that his characters should engage in disillusioned
analyses of collective pathology. It is collective pathology, not hered-
ity, the family, and social interrelationships with friends and acquain-
tances, which determines their own psychopathological, victimized
condition. The paradox of Comfort's novels is that the reader is often
presented with characters who are almost solipsistically driven inward because alienated from society and cut off from normal social
contacts, but characters whose thoughts and emotions are directed
outward. Power-centered institutions, not Comfort's rebellious protagonists, bear the burden of guilt. Consequently, his protagonists do
not experience depression—as the consequence of anger directed
against the self—or the anxiety of guilt, but anger against recogniza-
bly irresponsible institutions. As emotion gives expression to
thought, Comfort's protagonists, to explain themselves, their role as
victims, are driven to explain society.

It is Comfort's view of society which inhibits him from writing
conventional novels—after the manner of Fielding, Jane Austen,
Dickens, George Eliot—about characters interacting in society. His
characters usually cannot act within society, only react: by running,
by hostility, by engaging in unproductive acts of violence or nonvio-

lent resistance against society, and by explanations of the cause of their condition and, by extension, the human condition. It is also Comfort's view of society which inhibits his writing psychological novels in any conventional sense. The genius of the psychological novel, as in Camus's *The Fall* or Unamuno's *Abel Sanchez,* lies in the novelist's analysis of private motives, characters troubled by guilt and philosophically confused.

The problem of power in English literature has traditionally expressed itself in psychological studies of the will to power, as in Wordsworth's nihilistic anarchist, Oswald, of *The Borderers,* and in the works of Byron, Carlyle, and Lawrence. Among contemporary novelists C. P. Snow is most explicitly preoccupied with studies of power-loving personalities. Snow accepts a society in which the love of status, influence, and prestige are dominant motivations for human behavior. Comfort does not. For Snow, unlike Comfort, power is not in itself corrupting. His novels about power are essentially about the problem of class, the traditional source of dramatic conflict in English fiction since the modern novel's beginnings in Defoe, Fielding, and Richardson. Comfort avoids this source of dramatic tension.

Despite his interest in *Authority and Delinquency* in the psychology of power-loving personalities, Comfort is generally uninterested in his novels in depicting characters, such as Snow's Lewis Eliot, struggling for power and prestige. With the exception of Goggins in *Come Out to Play* (1961), who alone among Comfort's protagonists attains prestige within the framework of society, all of Comfort's protagonists are depicted in the process of losing the power to act effectively within society.

In contrast to conventional studies in English literature of the individual will to power, an interest in totalitarian power-structures develops in English fiction in the 1930s and 1940s. Such an interest develops along with the emergence of European fascism and with the disappearance of illusions concerning the essentially humane and progressive character of state socialism. Rex Warner in *The Professor* (1938) and *The Aerodrome* (1941) shows that he shares with Comfort a preoccupation with authoritarian social structures. But despite similarities, Warner is not working in the tradition in which Comfort is working. For Warner, "at the root" of the "whole cult of power and violence, including fascism, is the philosophy of the moral anarchist, of the individual asserting himself against general standards that seem too weak to be able to restrain him."[1] Unlike Comfort, Warner defends conventional values and democratic society against the encroachments of authoritarian regimes. Essentially the same may be said of Orwell, Koestler, and Greene in *The Power and the Glory*. But a fundamental resemblance exists between *The Professor*, *The Aerodrome*, *Darkness at Noon*, and *1984*, in particular, and the novels of Comfort. All present nightmarish visions of protagonists made powerless by impersonal authoritarian structures. Comfort's *A Giant's Strength* (1951) treats, as well, persecuted protagonists in conflict with misguided but idealistic—rather than merely power-loving—defenders of state socialism in a manner somewhat reminiscent of *The Power and the Glory*.

Huxley's novels, more than those of Warner, Orwell, Greene, or Koestler, resemble those of Comfort in their sociological focus and intimations, in *Island* and *Brave New World*, of decentralist alternatives to the modern democratic state. The " 'methods of dealing with the problems of power' " are explored in Huxley's *Island*. His utopian society is noncoercive, democratic, and evolved from " 'mutual aid [i.e., the principle of species solidarity and mutual assistance identified by Kropotkin in *Mutual Aid*, 1902] in a village community' " to " 'cooperative techniques of economics.' "[2]

Moreover, both Comfort and Huxley are preoccupied as novelists with the significance of sexual behavior to the individual and society and with the problems posed by science and technology. But Huxley often depicts a morality of sexual indulgence and the scientific method of analyzing experience and solving problems as threats to moral or spiritual values. In *Brave New World* both are also instruments of a future authoritarian society to enslave the masses. Comfort depicts the scientific mode of thinking and solving problems as a means of liberating society. In most of his novels (*No Such Liberty*, *The Almond Tree*, *The Power House* and *Come Out to Play*) he represents conventional and repressive sexual morality as the instrument of, and logical concomitant of, authoritarian society. Unlike Huxley, Comfort often presents protagonists who are scientists: Breitz in *No Such Liberty*, Hedler and Anosov in *A Giant's Strength*, Goggins in *Come Out to Play*, as well as Manson in *Cities of the Plain*. They are influenced in their political thinking by the scientific method (an intolerably reductionistic method as depicted in Huxley's novels). Moreover, they are sexually liberated and conspicuously cut off from conventional values and traditions without suffering from any accompanying sense of emptiness or disorientation.

The dynamics of mass psychology in Huxley's *Brave New World*, as evident, in particular, in his chapter-five description of the mystical experience of corporate existence, approximate the dynamics of mass psychology implied by Comfort's novels. For Huxley, as for Comfort, the fear of isolation motivates conformist behavior. But, more precisely, for Huxley it is the malaise of subjectivity which impels Huxley's protagonists towards mystical identification with others: a pathological, self-destructive identification in *Brave New World*, a self-fulfilling identification in *Island*. In Comfort's novels, personality is not intrinsically imprisoning, but is made imprisoning by a coercive society which alienates and isolates its members. Morever, Comfort's protagonists, in *No Such Liberty, The Power House, On This Side Nothing*, and *A Giant's Strength*, are literally imprisoned by society. The problem posed by the prison house of subjectivity, a preoccupation of French literature and Comfort in *The Almond Tree* and Book One of *The Power House*, is overshadowed by the more serious problem posed by literal imprisonment. In *On This Side Nothing*, Shmul Weinstock, Comfort's narrator, comes to think of imprisonment as "the occupational disease of the 20th century" (p. 131). His vision of the world is reminiscent of that of Vatlin in *The Power House*, who viewed society as an asylum, and Claus, the perpetual prisoner, who viewed the future as belonging to the "weak."

I   On This Side Nothing

On This Side Nothing (1949), a vigorous and imaginative account of political persecution, treats events transpiring before the end of World War II. Shmul Weinstock writes about his imprisonment in the Jewish ghetto of a North African city and, subsequently, in a British internment camp. Shmul arrives shortly before the ghetto is sealed off from the rest of the city by the Germans and Italians and witnesses its accidental bombardment by the British. He later becomes involved in a conspiracy to murder a young German soldier while a prisoner of the victorious British, is imprisoned for a short time in the old city jail, and manages to escape at the novel's conclusion. The novel develops less exhaustively, more economically, some of the themes of Comfort's more ambitious work, *The Power House*.

A serious problem of interpretation exists in several reviews which focus on the apparent negativism of the narrator, Shmul Weinstock. Impressed with the seemingly nihilistic implications of the novel's title, Bennel Braunstein in the *New York Herald Tribune Weekly Book Review* concluded that Shmul, "in the manner of the ancient tradition," was a "peddler" trying to sell

a spiritual drug. With it, he could anesthetize the world. But the world wouldn't buy and he became his own best customer. Being numb he could not fight but only think, and thinking, every thought was a question. What was civilization about, anyway? Was science really worth while? Where was the logic in death? What was a Jew?

For only one question would he essay an answer. He knew what a Jew was. . . . Beyond that, Shmul Weinstock saw nothing.[3]

Nothing in the novel supports such an interpretation. Shmul clearly believes that he knows what civilization is about, and he assumes that there is no logic in death. He is not a nihilist, and the title does not impute to Shmul, or Comfort, a nihilistic vision or perspective.

Mary Hurst in the *New York Times Book Review* arrived at a similarly mistaken conclusion. She argued that the novel was written by an author who "appears to have belief in nothing save the worth of the individual," and that Shmul represented "total nihilism." According to Hurst, Shmul does not identify himself with Rachel (a young Jewess to whom he is sexually attracted) because she believes "in taking action and escaping to Palestine."[4] Vernon Young's evaluation of the novel in the *Hudson Review* was similar:

He [Shmul] has arrogated to himself an identity of separateness which exists purely by negation. . . .

He refuses escape to Palestine with the comely young Jewess, Rachel, because she is already committed to the aims and content of the hive; childbearing and house-building are in her blood, instincts compromisingly communal. With the world upended for destruction, she is still wearing the Citizen-Face. She belongs, as Weinstock does not belong. . . . When the gregarious consciousness has been completely extirpated, it is difficult to imagine an object of dedication outside of oneself except art or God. Weinstock is an unlikely devotee of either, provided by Comfort with nothing but his one-track convictions.[5]

Mark Schorer added nothing significantly new to previous misinterpretations by arguing that the novel

shows us the social being as an empty shell when he has no authority with which to identify himself. . . . Mr. Comfort, as his title tells us, shows an adult recognizing the nothingness inside himself when he can no longer identify any of himself with the apparent something outside.

Its hero is a man who, with his last gasp of social impulse, rejoins his people, for whom he cares nothing.[6]

Serious literary criticism of the novel has been more perceptive. Burns, for example, noted that Schorer, "perhaps influenced by Vernon Young," has "misunderstood the novel from beginning to end. . . ."[7]

In a letter to Burns, Comfort explained that he picked "In dubious Battel" as the original title for his novel. He " 'then found that Steinbeck had used it' " and " 'looked a few lines farther for something else which would fit. . . .' " Burns suggested that the title implies that "we have all alike reduced modern life to a state of barbarism, until we are in Moloch's position. . . . That is, we have reached a final point: we are not in danger of falling in some future time, as in George Orwell's *1984*."[8] More generally, the title of *On This Side Nothing*, like that of *No Such Liberty*, suggests a state of powerlessness and entrapment. It fits Comfort's depiction of a world where soldiers are "busy farming with mines and rifles instead of turnips and forks," where a prison is a "factory for making nothing" (p. 174), and where Jews, on the wrong side of the wall which surrounds their ghetto, have nothing.

It is Shmul's sense of morality which distinguishes him from the seemingly nihilistic protagonists of writers such as Gide and Genet. Rebellion against common morality in Genet's autobiographical *The Thief's Journal* and Gide's *The Immoralist* originates in a longing for complete and spontaneous, or natural, fulfullment of the self. Shmul's rebellion has similar elements, but proceeds, fundamentally, from his ethical sense, his belief in the immorality of much conventional morality. The sense of delight in crime and sexual perversity, evident in Genet's works, is not to be found in Shmul's character. The narrator of *The Thief's Journal* finds excitement, he informs his readers, in assuming the role of "both victim and criminal."[9] Like Breitz in *No Such Liberty*, Shmul is unwillingly victimized by the Fascists and, subsequently, by the English. His identification with the criminal element of society develops largely from his being imprisoned like a criminal.

Perhaps nothing more strongly suggests Shmul's apparent nihilism than the kind of Nietzschean reversal of morality involved in his defense of social outcasts and criminals. Shmul explains to Goldberg:

If you have a culture which is a non-culture, you can't keep it going even if you want to, and the Jews and the bums and the jailbirds and the deserters start a new one under your feet that cracks your whole edifice like mushrooms cracking a pavement. (p. 149)

In the opening paragraphs of the novel Shmul remarks that Nicholides, the robber and dope peddler who smuggles him by sea and at night into the Jewish ghetto, is someone he can almost trust. Shmul goes on to conclude that it is easier to explain himself to a "scoundrel, a Homeric scoundrel" such as Nicholides (p. 9). Becoming implicated in a plot to assassinate Gellert (whose life he had earlier saved), Shmul explains to his readers his own unconventional views on assassination and murder:

I do not know why one should get excited about killing a man. It is not the most irresponsible thing we do—every time we vote for a government or obey someone, we do more to undermine decent living and human relationships than by killing someone who deserves it. . . . It is pretty safe to say that of the three sorts of killing—by war, by society (I mean the sort of killing by society which takes place when you starve someone or give him silicosis, not judicial execution), and by honest assassination with a dagger—the first two are always swindles, and the third usually is. Assassination or plain murder is the least immoral, and I can never see the logic which regards it as more cowardly than war—it is generally discriminate, and if there were any evidence that the right people were killed I could make a case for it. Usually it is Rosa Luxemburg they kill, not Titus Oates or General Franco, but at any rate it has a place as a means of dealing with tyrants. (pp. 155–56)

Shmul's attitude towards voting is partly the consequence of his conviction that democratic governments do not behave in a significantly better manner than fascist governments. After the ghetto is accidentally destroyed by English bombers, and the Jews are re-herded into an English internment camp, he observes that "in my own experience the color of the uniform doesn't make a great deal of difference" (p. 116). But even peacetime democracy is unacceptable. Sounding like Pierre Joseph Proudhon on democracy's tendency to multiply the number of sovereigns rather than to eliminate the principle of sovereignty, he argues, later, that the "Gentile democrats haven't killed their kings. . . ." Rather, they have "broken them up into small pieces and scattered them about. . ." (p. 134).

In sympathy with the criminal elements of society, Shmul is in opposition to "law and order," as conventionally defined by au-

thoritarian personalities both in and outside the ghetto. Commenting
on the successful political career of the turncoat Aldo (an Italian
policeman who retains his authority under the British), Shmul acidly
observes that Aldo and the policeman "belonged to the law and order
apparatus and mattered more than fresh water or housing or hospi-
tals" (p. 120). Shmul's imprisonment by the British reinforces his
antipathy towards social organizations based on law and order. He
escapes from prison at the novel's conclusion partly in order to avoid
contributing to the mechanical "law and order apparatus" by which
Gellert's assassins are to be prosecuted (p. 184). The physical destruction of the ghetto by the British and the social chaos engendered by
both the Fascists and the British should be understood by the reader
as illustrating that the philosophy of law and order breeds disorder.

Genuine morality for Shmul does not depend on law or punishments, and he finds in the Jewish disbelief in immortality, and
attendant rewards and punishments, a model for morality in secular
society. Alluding to the Sadducees' disbelief in immortality, to
Lucretius's Epicurean materialism which made belief in immortality
impossible, and to Plato's concept of immortality which rivals that of
Christianity, Shmul informs his readers,

We were the first to find out that you did not need a promise of canings and
prizegivings like a school class to retain your human solidarity and your desire
to deal justly. The first Sadducees were Jews. Even Plato couldn't hold a
candle to that—he had a shamefast, depersonalized heaven of his own.
Lucretius must have been a Jew, one of my Jews. (p. 44)

The novel implies that the alternative to order guaranteed by a law
and order apparatus is order guaranteed by individual rationality and
responsibility. In this respect the implications of *On This Side
Nothing* are similar to those of Herbert Read's *The Parliament of
Women*. Read's protagonist, Helena, responding to Anna's defense of
coercive order within society, says, "But do not call this God's design,
which I would rather seek in my own heart than in a prince's court."[10]

In its treatment of the ruinous effects of the law-and-order apparatus on the individual and society generally, *On This Side Nothing*
is also anticipated by Read's *The Green Child*. Stimulated by such
liberal philosophers as Voltaire, Rousseau, and Diderot, Olivero
develops his "Articles of Government" to provide Roncador with a
comprehensive legal system and constitution. The movement of
Roncador towards a dictatorship indicates, among other thing, that

even the most idealistically conceived law-and-order apparatus tends naturally to degenerate into rigid, life-negating authoritarianism. In the underground world of *The Green Child*, by way of contrast, a law-and-order apparatus does not exist, for such an apparatus depends upon the written codification of moral abstractions. Read's underground beings had "never conceived the idea of writing" and their language is "devoid of abstract concepts."[11] A similar antithesis exists in Henry Treece's *How I See Apocalypse*. Influenced by the anarchism of Read, Treece argues that Apocalypticism is a mode of living in which "natural law takes over from man-made law," and that man-made law is a "ready-made contraption . . . imposed from above by the powerful. . . ."[12]

Like *The Power House, On This Side Nothing* depicts a society in which distinctions in wealth and property are guaranteed by law, and in which such distinctions contribute to the fragmentation of society. The sealing off of the ghetto from the rest of the city by the law-and-order apparatus has the effect of further fragmenting society generally. But it simultaneously creates a situation within the ghetto in which a law-and-order apparatus is not functioning and which, consequently, provides new possibilities for social organization. Speaking of the peasant Jews who have been herded into the ghetto, Shmul describes what happens at the house of his father:

The newcomers appeared silently on the stairs, put down their belongings, and settled, without a word. . . . They had come to stay. . . . Weinstock looked over his shoulder down the stairway. It was full of bundles and of people, and he could tell one from another, they were all so shapeless and immobile, only by the flock of eyes. A baby was being quietly suckled near his right foot. It too fixed its eyes on him. A woman lower down was mixing oatmeal in an earthen pot. Notes from a wireless set in the boarding-house opposite drifted in the dark stairway, and there was a powerful unclean smell that made my father feel sick. One of the children saluted him gravely.

By the time he had got me downstairs and begun to ask for explanations, a wood fire was burning on his landing and a piece of something was cooking. The smoke blew in long puffs across the bedroom.

And they sat there, the expatriates—they had come to stay. Sheets and partitions of old carpet and blanket divided the stairway into cubicles. Archways and doorways were colonized. Throughout the whole district it was the same. Only the few professional families, who had forgotten how to go into exile, wandered about looking for hospitality. The poor had never lost touch with the knowledge of dispossession which circulated in their blood—like xerophytic plants they had taken up their roots and moved on. The lawyer, Babinski, who had heard about me was coming to call: he had been to the gate to argue and expostulate with the picket there, and read the notices which they had posted; he stood at the foot of the stairs before going up and looked at this encrustation of humanity which had settled overnight, like a drift of leaves. . . .

Babinski yelled down the stairs, "Get out, you bums! Out!" Nobody moved. (pp. 19–21)

The response above of Babinski, the lawyer, is respectful of the law-and-order apparatus and disrespectful to those who breach authority, and is conventionally rational and liberal, with argument and expostulation taking the place of direct action. The response of the "professional families" is similar. Shmul contrasts such conventional responses to authority and social inequality with that of the uncivilized peasant Jews who know intuitively the art of expropriation. As compared with the symbolically suggestive conclusion of *Cities of the Plain*, the phenomenon of dispossession depicted above involves the expropriation of the articles of consumption rather than the means of production. (Kropotkin went beyond conventional socialist theory in advocating the expropriation of both.) That Shmul identifies with the peasant Jews who colonize his father's house is indicated by his referring to them in the same language that he uses in referring to himself—as "expatriates" and children of the "exile."

Shmul's sense of exile and identification with the nomadic peasant class is linked with his anarchist rejection of government. He does not reject Rachel and does not escape with her to Palestine simply because she believes in "taking action" (as Hurst argues) or because he lacks a "gregarious" or "communal" sense (as Vernon Young argues). Palestine is not a viable alternative for him because he does not wish to back "the notion that freedom is something national" (p. 45). Freedom with responsibility is impossible for Shmul as a member of any state. When Rachel says to him that the "only Jewish part of you is your face" and that he belongs "to the Exile," Shmul responds by asserting that he "personally would go on being a Jew long after there was nothing in the world but Exile" (p. 188). He apparently finds in the two-thousand-year history of Jewish statelessness a symbol of his own anarchist, self-imposed exile from all states. The sea, a traditional symbol of exile and loneliness, is employed by Comfort to reinforce the image of Shmul as exile and to give the novel a kind of circular shape. Shmul arrives by sea at the beginning of the novel and resumes his perennial wanderings by taking to the sea again at its conclusion.

In its treatment of an exile and fugitive who feels compelled to return to his homeland, and escapes again at the novel's conclusion, *On This Side Nothing* resembles Silone's *Bread and Wine*. Like that of Silone's Pietro Spina, Shmul's unending exile is a symbolic expression of his developing revolutionary consciousness which—to be maintained in an uncorrupted state—must be disengaged from political and ecclesiastical authority and party ideology and discipline.

The protagonists of Comfort's novels, as noted by John Doheney in "Alex Comfort as Novelist," are nearly all "victims—wafted this way and that by war, almost always running or hiding."[13] The pattern of escape, flight, and pursuit which characterizes some of Comfort's fiction may owe something to Godwin's remarkably effective use of such a narrative pattern in *Caleb Williams*. But it is partly the particular perspective of anarchist thought—its assumption that the individual is in a life-and-death conflict with grotesque institutions and irrational, irresponsible public officials—which largely determines such a pattern. It determines as well Comfort's and Godwin's vision of the protagonist as victim. Where persecution because of antigovernmental beliefs becomes an impending possibility, there is added reason for the interest of anarchist writers in creating imaginative accounts of escape, flight, and pursuit. Godwin wrote under Pitt's administration immediately after the French Revolution. Comfort writes during the emotional fervor of the Second World War. But even in works written about "anarchists" by writers who are not anarchists, the pattern of victimization—or paranoia, depending partly on the point of view—and pursuit is likely to develop naturally. Such a pattern is evident in Conrad's *The Secret Agent* and Chesterton's *The Man Who Was Thursday*, which culminates in the madcap pursuit of Sunday, the alleged anarchist ringleader of Chesterton's novel.[14]

As victimized rebels, Comfort's protagonists find their counterparts in the underground figures of Dostoevski and Ralph Ellison, in Sartre's Orestes and in Camus's Sisyphus, but primarily in the protagonists of other anarchist writers. Anosov in *A Giant's Strength*, Breitz in *No Such Liberty*, Claus in *The Power House* and Shmul in *On This Side Nothing* are anticipated by Godwin's Imogen and Caleb Williams, Read's Green Child, and Shelley's Prometheus. All are persecuted, harried and locked up, imprisoned, by persons who symbolize or represent irrational forms of authority. The victimized protagonists of Godwin's *Imogen*, Read's *The Green Child*, and Shelley's *Prometheus Unbound* are protagonists whose unbinding means the restoration of a society not founded upon the principle of power or coercion. The protagonists of Comfort's first five novels are always unable to achieve any kind of decisive victory over authoritarian society because they are presented realistically rather than as characters in allegory or fantasy. In *Come Out to Play*, a fantasy, Comfort's protagonist functions as a kind of Promethean figure, a fire-bringer, who liberates mankind with an illuminating, liberalizing chemical substance (named "3-blindmycin" by Goggins).

A sense of exile, victimization, entrapment, powerlessness, isolation, alienation, anxiety, and unending frustration characterize much of Comfort's art, but is more explicitly revealed in his novels. Such motifs also characterize Kafka's works in which, similarly, the autobiographical element is strong. The Apocalyptic writers claimed Kafka as one of their precursors, and a Kafkaesque atmosphere permeates much of the early poetry and fiction of Hendry and Treece. Consequently, the Kafkaesque quality of Comfort's fiction may be said to be influenced in part by his acquaintance with and admiration for Apocalyptic literature, as well as influenced by the general interest in Kafka which emerged in the 1930s and 1940s. There are, however, essential differences between Kafka's fiction and Comfort's. In *Darwin and the Naked Lady* Comfort argues that there is a kind of novel, distinguished from the "social novel" and the "picaresque novel," which is

getting common, and which it is hard at times to avoid writing: that is the novel which is realistic, but the reality which it depicts is fantasy come to life and enacted in history. In our life time a writer possessed by a fantasy—the obsessive-compulsive fantasy of Kafka, for example, or the sadistic fantasy of Mirbeau—does not need to invent a situation in which it can be expressed; other similarly preoccupied people in positions of authority are already expressing these fantasies in current affairs. Kafka depicting his prison camp, digging his burrow, or trying to get into the castle is relying on his imagination, but today he could equally well be writing documentaries. (p. 95)

Several critics have called attention to some Kafkaesque elements in Comfort's fiction. Harold Drasdo has observed that "Behind Bars" has "the horror of 'In a Penal Settlement.' "[15] Mark Schorer in the *Kenyon Review* has commented on the "incorporation of Kafka-like symbols (walls, tunnels, the alien, the prisoner, exile, etc.) in a naturalistic method" in *On This Side Nothing*. But Schorer has argued as well that such symbols are "the by now familiar trapping of our fiction, our mythologizing short-cuts to a large perception."[16]

Better insights along this line have been made by Wayne Burns in
his analysis of *On This Side Nothing*, in which he argues that the novel
is "an authentic realistic counterpart of Kafka's" *In The Penal
Colony*—"a rewriting of *In The Penal Colony* for our time." Burns
notes that Kafka's world

is the world we live in when our "egos" are trying to come to terms with our
"superegos." The conflict is nearly always between some form of "I" and what
seems to be actuality, but which is actuality as it has been shaped and
patterned by the super-ego. For this reason, Kafka's heroes move in a world,
not of ordinary reality, but of reality submerged in nightmare, a world
peopled not with the ordinary characters of any type of fiction, but with
human or animal representatives of the forces of the super-ego. And these
forces, dressed up like men or animals, appear and act in his fiction as they
appear and act to the beleaguered ego: as having right, and might, and
therefore sanity. So that the "I" has no choice but to conform—either that, or
be destroyed.
. . . .
    In The Penal Colony . . . depicts a totally different order of reality from
that which *On This Side Nothing* explores: the sub-real as opposed to the
surface-real, the latent as opposed to the manifest content of our civilization.[17]

Such conclusions by Burns, which he confines to *On This Side
Nothing*, as well as Comfort's conclusions above, are applicable to
much of Comfort's fiction, especially *No Such Liberty, The Power
House, A Giant's Strength*, and *On This Side Nothing*.
    Among Comfort's novels *No Such Liberty* most clearly foreshadows
On This Side Nothing in grim images and descriptions suggesting
uncertainty and entrapment. The uncertainty and confusion of Breitz
in *No Such Liberty*, Serge in *The Almond Tree*, and Fougueux in
Book One of *The Power House* originate in the uncertainty of their
predicament as victims of society or a meaningless, contingent
universe. But uncertainty, confusion, and bewilderment concerning
the character of society and the universe are usually not fixed
elements in the personalities of Comfort's protagonists. Especially in
the later novels they develop the sort of confidence in their own
intellectual abilities to penetrate the ambiguous and confusing surface of external reality that is denied to Kafka's protagonists.
    Kafka took external authority seriously and internalized it, as Burns
(above) and other Kafka critics have suggested. More specifically,
Kafka, it is now recognized, took seriously the authority of his father,

as indicated by his letters[18] and expressed most clearly in his short story "The Judgment." Comfort, whose *The Silver River* indicates that he got along well with his father, had no similar personal, autobiographical motivations for writing. His protagonists, with the exception (to some degree) of those of *The Almond Tree*, in which the authority of the father—the patriarch Pyotr—has been thoroughly internalized, are never deeply troubled by feelings of self-rejection and self-condemnation. Unlike Kafka's protagonists they discover that the demands of the conscience are not ambiguous, and discover, especially in the last four novels, that external absurdity need not lead to internal confusion. Unlike Kafka's "K," or for that matter Hardy's Jude, none is knocking at the doors of the establishment, seeking recognition, acceptance, and redemption.

Robert Key in *The Spectator* briefly noted that the scene of *On This Side Nothing* is "set in north Africa, but it is not only this that recalls Camus's *The Plague*."[19] Comfort's fiction generally resembles that of Camus. Perhaps more than any other European writer during the 1940s, Camus is similarly preoccupied in his art with the problems posed by power and the absurdity of death as the consequence of man's existence in a hostile universe. The conflict against death is for Comfort a "conflict against the Universe" (in the language of *Art and Social Responsibility*). Some of his protagonists, like their creator, struggle against creation as physicians: Breitz in *No Such Liberty;* the young physician in *Into Egypt;* and, especially, Manson in *Cities of the Plain*. The literal level of *The Plague*, an allegory, signifies Camus's moral concerning the problem of death. The narrator paraphrases Dr. Rieux's responses to Tarrou's questions concerning the doctor's lack of religious faith:

His face still in shadow, Rieux said that he'd already answered: that if he believed in an all-powerful God he would cease curing the sick and leave that to Him. . . . Anyhow, in this respect Rieux believed himself to be on the right road—in fighting against creation as he found it.[20]

The Plague is also an allegory about fascism. But as Camus himself observes in a letter to Roland Barthes, its allegorical vagueness (for which the novel was criticized) allows it to "apply to any resistance against any tyranny."[21]

On This Side Nothing nonallegorically demonstrates the necessity of man's unending struggle against all forms of political tyranny, as well as against the tyranny of death. Born in Algiers, Camus writes about what he knows. Comfort, as in all of his novels, relies essentially on secondhand knowledge. But Camus's *The Plague*, published two years earlier, may have given dimension to Comfort's imagination. As in *The Plague* the town gates are locked, forcing the entrapped citizens into confrontations with the elemental realities of physical suffering, isolation, and death. Shmul's developing awareness links him with Camus's Rieux and Rambert, who discover in similar circumstances the necessity for human solidarity in the face of external threats, whether physical or political, to survival. In Comfort's next novel, *A Giant's Strength*, his protagonist, Hedler, similarly develops a sense of human solidarity. However, he is not isolated and entrapped in a city, but in a desert which forces confrontation with the elemental realities of survival in a hostile environment, or, on a symbolic level, a universe indifferent to man's struggle to exist. But less thoroughly redeemed from the plague of cultural barbarism than Camus's Dr. Rieux, Comfort's protagonists, Shmul and Hedler, to some extent find their counterparts also—if not their partial inspiration—in the highly perceptive but amoral protagonist of Camus's *The Stranger*.

In *The Novel and Our Time* Comfort provides an analysis of Camus's *The Stranger* that Wayne Booth has described as "an excellent discussion of the problems raised for the reader by this [Camus's] puzzling work."[22] Comfort writes that

One of the most striking examples of an inacceptable hero who is being presented critically to the reader as a means of explaining his conduct is Mersault [*sic*] in Camus's *The Outsider*. The problem here is to explain the actions and attitudes of a man who has one of the chief attributes of barbarian civilizations—deficient response to any normal emotion, resulting from the mischief done to him by his childhood in an asocial society. He is also a schizoid psychopath, but most of his conduct is due to the suppression of affect which goes with the horizonless, purposeless, unorientated life of modern society.

This kind of problem is typical of the contemporary novel, with the background of technical and scientific awareness which it has derived from psychology, and the rootless, shiftless society in which it exits. There is something in common between Mersault and Jean Valjean, but Camus understands his character, while Hugo sympathizes with his. . . .

Those who read about Mersault will fall into one of three groups, all of which Camus must have been able to foresee: Those who resent the whole book; those who understand Mersault as well as Camus does, and applaud the book because of its insight; and those who detect in their own personality the affectlessness and psychopathy of the man who is describing himself and react by disquiet, a measure of comprehension, and thought. (pp. 41–43)

Most of the characters appearing in Comfort's first five novels suffer a loss of spontaneity and affective depth by virtue of existing in the sort of "horizonless, purposeless, unoriented" society which Comfort describes above. In particular, Shmul in *On This Side Nothing* and Hedler in *A Giant's Strength* recall Camus's Meursault, for both manifest deficient responses with respect to what Comfort above classifies as "normal emotion." Shmul accepts a passive role in the assassination of Gellert, is unable to respond sexually and emotionally to Rachel, and is not deeply affected by the death of his father. Escaping from the Russians by plane, Hedler kills his pilot while they are flying over a mideastern desert. His failure to respond emotionally to the pilot's death with remorse, compassion or regret is reminiscent of Meursault's inability to respond emotionally to his mother's death and the death of the Arab whom he kills. But unlike Meursault, Shmul and Hedler develop a sense of moral responsibility while manifesting at the same time emotional deficiencies.

II   A Giant's Strength

Published in 1952, *A Giant's Strength* is about Cold-War politics. Like that of *On This Side Nothing*, its title suggests Comfort's continuing interest in the problem of power. Julius Hedler, a German who by the age of twenty-one has become an authority on "calculating machines" or computers, is exploited during the Second World War by the Germans, who discover that his talents have significance to their rocket technology. After the end of the war he becomes the property of the Americans, who are also interested in his mathematical abilities, but escapes to the eastern zone of Berlin in 1947. He is taken to the University of Tashkent, where he discovers that the Russians also intend to exploit his talents. Tired of being manipulated, he hopes to escape by plane "to Persia, or any other country where he would be indispensable to nobody," but, having killed his noncompliant pilot, finds himself stranded in the Turkestan desert. He is overtaken, at the novel's conclusion, by a Soviet scientific expedition. Shemirin, the leader of the expedition, has been Hedler's colleague and friend. He allows Hedler to escape after making him promise that "under no circumstances" will he work for the enemy, those whom Shemirin calls "imperialist warmongers."

During the course of the expedition, Shemirin discusses politics with Anosov, a Kropotkinian anarchist and geologist who serves as a guide for the expedition. *A Giant's Strength* is a novel of ideas in which its major characters, Hedler, Anosov, and Shemirin, function as spokesmen for different philosophical points of view. Hedler sometimes functions as Comfort's spokesman. Anosov expresses Kropotkinian ideas in his discussions with Shemirin, who defends Soviet Communism.

The appearance of Major Serkin in chapter three provides the novel with some of the characteristics of a detective story. Beginning with his discussion with Edgeworth (a British journalist who later defects) in chapter three, Serkin dutifully attempts to unravel the mystery of Hedler's disappearance. Discovering at Tashkent Hedler's letters to Shemirin, Serkin is provided with an opportunity to analyze Hedler's motivations. Hedler's letters, in turn, provide Comfort an opportunity to incorporate into the novel some of his own reflections on the possible significance of computers to the problem of government. Halfway through one of the letters, Serkin comes upon a "passage that fixed his attention." Hedler has written:

"In the matter of the machine. I have wondered, since I came to look at things in the way I have described, whether the machine itself is not the ultimate solution. As you know, it is theoretically possible to construct a machine capable of arriving at judgments. If we can provide such a machine with the factual material, it is both logical and inerrant. It does not deteriorate by the exercise of its function, it could represent a complete disembodiment of the integrative power of the State, a completely translucent and disinterested machine, capable of its own species of wisdom, incorruptible, unambitious. It could be idolized with safety, pursuing without falsification the programme laid down in its structure, able to exercise mercy and judgment. We should have to punch the cards which determine that program. Would that be impossible, in the terms that I have stated? Could we define the terms? Humanity has defined them frequently and amply—in the Constitution of the United States, in your own constitution—would that satisfy you?" (pp. 199–200)

Similar conclusions are embodied in the revised 1970 edition of Comfort's *Authority and Delinquency* in which the constitutions of the United States and the USSR are also cited as possibly providing the terms by which the computer might be programmed:

The possible role of judgment-making computing machines in replacing

political authority is a less alarming and less foolish idea than it appears at first
sight to be. . . .

The Constitutions of the U.S.A. or the USSR, *if they were actually put into
effect*, would give a very plausible semblance of public justice. A computer
which implemented the Constitution of the United Nations and the Declara-
tion of Human Rights, by turning off the electricity in defector states, would
greatly improve the conduct of exisiting governments. (p. 86)

Serkin, reading Hedler's letter, thinks it must be some sort of
"private joke" (p. 200). Comfort in *Authority and Delinquency* notes
that his suggestions concerning computerized government "are
closer to satire than to possibility, but they cannot be discounted
entirely." He goes on to argue that the "principle of replacing
judgment by computation in cases where it is subject to large
personal biases is a valid one, of which we may hear more" (pp.
86–87).

Chapter fourteen incorporates a discussion between Anosov and
Shemirin reminiscent of the extended philosophical discussions of
Huxley's novels of ideas. After the expedition has made camp,
Shemirin, captivated by Anosov's reserve in expressing himself,
begins a conversation. The two soon discover that they have at least
"one thing in common"—they have both been prisoners. Shemirin
tells of being imprisoned by the Germans. Anosov recounts his
experience as a student during and after the Revolution. He had been
happy living in Moscow after the Revolution, but, losing his room
after being hospitalized, had decided to go to Dimitrov. There he
lives in the house of Peter Kropotkin. Anosov tells Shemirin that he
had angrily suggested to Kropotkin that his anarchist beliefs kept him
from facing realistically the changes that were occurring in Russia (a
charge which Shemirin had made against Anosov). He goes on to
relate,

"And if I was angry with him, he was white with anger against us, anger and
grief. It had been announced that day that we were taking hostages from
Wrangel's army, to try to stop some of the things those devils were doing to
our people. And he said to me: 'You're a Bolshevik: what sort of beginning is
this? If you do this now, how soon will you resort to torture, as in the Middle
Ages?' " (p. 159)

Anosov adds, "He wrote to Lenin, in the terms he spoke to me."

The real Kropotkin did return to Dimitrov after the revolution,
and, on the twenty-first of December, 1920, wrote to Lenin:

An announcement has been placed in *Izvestiia* and in *Pravda* which makes known the decisions of the Soviet government to seize as hostages SRs (Social Revolutionary party members) from the Savinkov and Chernov groups, White Guards of the nationalist and tactical center, and Wrangel officers; and in case of an (assassination) attempt on the leaders of the soviets, to "mercilessly exterminate" these hostages.

Is there really no one around you to remind your comrades and to persuade them that such measures represent a return to the worst period of the Middle Ages and religious wars, and are undeserving of people who have taken it upon themselves to create a future society on communist principles?[23]

The historical perspective given to the discussion by both Shemirin and Anosov, as well as its historicity, furthers its abstract character as an exploration of the similarities and differences between Soviet communism and Kropotkinian anarchism. On the immediate level of characterization, such fictionalized historical information indicates the genesis of personality development. Character is defined historically in *A Giant's Strength*, rather than from the perspective of the immediate environment, as in *The Power House*. The immediate environment does not so much determine the behavior of Anosov, Shemirin, and Hedler as strengthen and delineate character traits developed decades before their story begins.

As compared with Koestler's *Darkness at Noon* or Orwell's *Animal Farm*, *A Giant's Strength* presents a relatively sympathetic view of Soviet communism. The dialogue between Shemirin and Anosov is followed by a skirmish between the nomads who have captured Hedler and Shemirin's expeditionary group. Hedler is abandoned by the nomads, held prisoner by Shemirin and his coworkers, and finally released. The novel concludes:

Hedler, from the saddle, leaned over and held out his hand to Shemirin. "We're not enemies," he said. Shemirin took it. "Remember your promise," he said. From the rock he watched the horse go out of sight.

The epigraph of the novel reads, "—O brother Montagu: give me thy hand." Like much British and European literature of the 1940s and 1950s, *A Giant's Strength* represents, in part, a defense of the individual against the tyranny of abstract political thought. Yet in a period in which intellectuals were lamenting and lambasting a god that had failed, Comfort unconventionally avoids envisioning Soviet society in a manner which would encourage the pervasive Cold-War atmosphere of hostility and unbridled distrust.

III   Come Out to Play

Come Out to Play (1961), Comfort's latest novel, is, as Harold Drasdo has observed, "Comfort's first venture into comedy."[24] More precisely, it is his first such venture in novel form. *Come Out to Play* has a distant analogue in the most humorous of his short stories of the 1940s, "A Citizen with Thirty-Nine Vertebrae."

The novel's narrator, Dr. George Goggins, returns to Paris after working for six years on the problem of population for the Indian government. "Stranded in Paris without a paying job, he has only three assets—a sound practical and theoretical knowledge of human mating habits, the capacity to 'sell boots to fish,' and Dulcinea. Dulcinea is beautiful (of course) and it occurs to Goggins that if he and she can please each other with such virtuosity, they can teach other people to do likewise. He founds a school for NATO expatriates." But "Aristophanic complications" develop. " 'Togetherness' sweeps the Top People. . . . The Press is flannelled. . . . In the thick of the uproar is the genially insufferable Goggins, dealing out Sanskrit, Freud, chemistry, information, love and codology in all directions."[25]

If the novel were to be made into a movie, Comfort would like to see Peter Sellers play Goggins and Sophia Loren play Dulcinea.[26] Goggins and Dulcinea combine comedy, intellect, and assertion of personality. Comfort sees them as a "Beatrice and Benedict couple" (Shakespeare's *Much Ado About Nothing*). He also sees Goggins as "occasionally . . . John Tanner"[27] (the anarchic hero of Shaw's *Man and Superman* who meets his match in Ann Whitefield). Goggins is partly autobiographical. Like Comfort, he has lived in Ireland for a while, has specialized knowledge about Indian culture and sexual behavior, and has taught physiology. Like Comfort, he is a physician, a biologist, and "an international expert on human mating behavior" (p. 49). Both are apparently high-dominance personalities. ("I think in general people of high dominance experimentally have been shown to be prepared to try almost anything once," Comfort observes.[28]) Comfort "wasn't aware" of Goggins as a "self-portrait" at the time the novel was written. But Goggins, he explains, is the "only character in my novels who bears the smallest resemblance to me. As one lady recently told me, I tend to alternate between being Ferdinand and being the Minotaur." Goggins was somewhat "like that." He was partly "from the soul. And I've actually been a little afraid to act it [the novel] out, although we [presumably Comfort and Jane, his present wife] have done nearly all of it."[29]

It is of significance with respect to Comfort's development, as well as to his recent "futurological" interests at the Institute for Higher Studies (in Santa Barbara, California), that the novel is in several respects anticipatory. For example, the relationship between Goggins and Dulcinea provides a pattern for what might now be described as an "open marriage." According to Comfort, Goggins's and Dulcinea's relationship "is Frederick Perls's primary relationship: 'I am I and you are you, and neither of us is here to live up to the other one's expectations. But when we do, it's beautiful.' "[30] Neither exploitative nor possessional, Goggins's and Dulcinea's relationship includes the possibility of subsidiary relationships. Goggins explains to Dulcinea (who, like Shaw's Ann Whitefield, desires the security of the marriage contract) that there is "no absolute rule now that one only dances with one's lifetime partner—though one may do just that for preference when she dances as beautifully as Dulcinea" (p. 65). Dulcinea comes to decide, "I don't care about forsaking all others, but don't forsake me" (p. 67).

In "Sexuality in a Zero Growth Society" (1974), Comfort writes, "I would expect . . . to see a society in which pair relationships are still central, but initially less permanent, in which childbearing is seen as a special responsibility involving a special life style, and in which settled couples engage openly in a wide range of sexual relations with friends, with other couples, and with third parties as an expression of social intimacy, without prejudice to the primacy of their own relationships, and with no more, and probably less, permanent interchange than we see in the society of serial polygamy with adultery that now exists. Such a pattern is coming into existence in America, and is beginning to become explicit."[31]

Comfort's exploration of communication through odors in *Come Out to Play* is also anticipatory. Marcel, a chemist, is influenced by an article Goggins had earlier published on the possibility of producing "substances which would act like long-range hormones." Marcel discovers two new chemical fragrances. One is named Cocuficin because it "makes you feel as if you had been cuckolded." It evokes hostility and resentment from males. The other is called 3-blindmycin by Goggins—they "all ran after the farmer's wife." It is a potent aphrodisiac. In the "Author's Note" for the 1975 edition of the novel, Comfort writes that much of the "literature research which went into COTP ended up as a review in *Nature*."

Some of the research apparently also ended up in Comfort's "Communication May be Odorous" in *New Scientist and Science*

Journal (1971). In the essay Comfort writes that "science fiction has
an awkward way of coming true. Nearly 10 years back I wrote a
science fiction novel which turned about the discovery, use and abuse
of human pheromones. A pheromone is a substance secreted by one
individual which affects the behaviour of another—an olfactory hor-
mone. . . . The main aim of the book was political satire, but the
biology   unfortunately   took   over—only   biochemists   and
psychoanalysts found it funny. . . ." As one example of odorous
communication in humans, Comfort cites the work of M. C.
Kalogerakis and L. Bieber which indicates that "odour plays an
important part in infantile psychosexual development. At the stage in
development when dominance-competition between son and father
appears, the 'oedipal phase'; it is accompanied by a marked awareness
of the sexual odour of adults, with distaste for that of the same-sex
parent." Comfort goes on to observe that a "biological psychoanalyst
could not fail to note that three regions in man are provided with
odour glands and large, odour-diffusing hair tufts—the breast-axilla
complex, and the anal and the genital regions, all imprinting points in
human development." But olfactory sensitivity, which "varies greatly
in humans," is apparently repressed for psychosexual reasons, although "the variation is at least in part genetic."[32]

Also anticipatory is Comfort's presentation in *Come Out to Play* of a
clinic for sexual behavior. The "Publishers Note" in the 1975 edition
of the novel makes the point that "not long after this imaginative
flight, the first sex clinic was founded by Masters and Johnson,
followed by many others of similar nature. All could have been
patterned after the pioneer effort of Dr. George Goggins and Dulcinea McGredy." Essentially the same point is made by Masters and
Johnson themselves, as recorded in Patrick McGrady's *The Love
Doctors*. While interviewing Masters and Johnson, McGrady men-
tioned Comfort:

"Comfort is so much fun," said Mrs. Johnson. "If we could learn to produce
on a twenty-four-hour-day level the way he does, I think we'd probably have
it made. I just get so exhausted."
"Five or six hours is all I can stand," added Masters. "I end up out of breath
while he's talking. He wrote a parody on the type of thing we're doing—
before he knew about us. It was a delightful little farce, but it happened to
have a helluva lot of clinical application. But he didn't know it at the time."[33]

The novel also anticipates *The Joy of Sex* (1972). The novel's droll
chapter headings ("The Owl and the Pussy-Cat," "The Cat and the

Fiddle," "In Which England Expects," and "In Which the Cow
Jumps Over the Moon") prefigure those of *The Joy of Sex,* which
make palatable Comfort's libertarian conclusions about sexual behavior with culinary, rather than nursery-rhyme, references: "Start-
ers," "Main Courses," and "Sauces and Pickles." More significantly,
however, Goggins's ideas about sexual behavior are anticipatory.
According to Comfort in a cover note for the 1975 edition of the novel,
"*Come Out to Play* started to be simply a comic novel. I think now it
was the manifesto of which *The Joy of Sex* commences the implementation." In the novel Goggins, lamenting the turndown rate for the
course at the sex clinic, tells Chandra (an Indian psychiatrist who
assists Goggins in his clinic), " 'If only we could keep the other fifty
percent . . . it might begin to be important. If we motivate the
stayers-away, it would be really revolutionary—we should have set
out to teach a sport [Cordon Bleu sex] and ended by saving civilization; naturally it won't work' " (pp. 119–20). Earlier, Goggins explains his purpose to Dulcinea: " 'We would give these people, if they
were able to take it, their first real experience of pleasure, and see if it
helped them or civilized them at all. I expected that quite half the
benefit would come, not from any techniques we could teach them,
but simply from the sense of permission implied in being taught' "
(p. 50).

In his introduction to his translation of *The Koka Shastra*, Comfort
writes that "the main social function of erotic literature is in cultivat-
ing a sense of permission and overcoming sexual anxiety, rather than
in imparting specific information" (p. 94). To the extent that it does
so, erotic literature in general, like Goggins's sex clinic, is potentially
therapeutic and humanizing. Moreover, nonrepressive and relational sexuality is for Comfort to some extent a correlate of social
justice. "You can't have good sex unless you've gotten a reasonable
degree of social justice. At the moment it tends to be confined to the
prosperous. And one of the first things people who have come to
discover good sex are going to want is to be able to have some privacy
and to have some prosperity. They are not going to want to be hauled
off to fight against people they never saw. . . . I think there is nothing
like a good sex life to make you into a militant radical—to make
ordinary people militant, mind you, not just exponent radicals who
may be using their radicalism as a substitute for sex. The problem is to
radicalize the public as a whole, people who wouldn't normally think
of themselves as radicals, the sort of people who turned out against
the Suez war in England, and the only thing they could think of to

sing was 'Auld Lang Syne' because they didn't know any political
songs. When you get those people marching, the government is in
trouble."[34]

Pleasureable (that is, joyful or playful) sexual behavior is potentially therapeutic, radicalizing, and a correlate of social justice. The
planned and essential purpose of *The Joy of Sex* was neither revolutionary nor psychiatric. To the extent that it fosters Cordon Bleu
sex ("good sex"), however, it assists in the implementation of Goggins's or Comfort's theories in the novel. In 1974 Comfort was asked,
"Would it be accurate to assume that your latest works represent in
part the conviction that sexual liberalization leads to social liberalization, or, as the behaviorists might put it, that behavior modification in
one area is liable to be generalized to other areas?" He responded,
"Yes, I think it's probably true. But that wasn't why I did it [*The Joy of
Sex* or *More Joy*]. I did it partly because I thought the sex thing
needed doing for itself. There wasn't a book based on the knowledge
of 1974. They were all based on the knowledge of 1874. I thought it
was time we did one. . . ." But he went on to repeat, "I think that's
true, in fact; it probably does happen."[35] And in *The Joy of Sex*
Comfort writes, "If we were able to transmit the sense of play which is
essential to a full, enterprising, and healthily immature view of sex
between committed people, we would be performing a mitzvah:
people who play flagellation games and are excited by them bother
nobody, provided they don't turn off a partner who finds the scenario
frightening. People who enact similar aggressions outside the bedroom are apt to end up at My Lai or Belsen. The aim of this book is
pleasure, not psychiatry, but we suspect that the two coincide. Play is
one function of sexual elaboration—playfulness is a part of love which
could well be the major contribution of the Aquarian revolution to
human happiness" (p. 13).

The problem with the authoritarian characters that Goggins deals
with in the novel is that they do enact similar aggressions outside the
bedroom. Unable to discharge their anxieties and aggressions in
coital play, they play the more dangerous and destructive games of
coercive society. Chandra tells Goggins that Fundament, the
Foreign Secretary, "is governing the world out of his nursery like the
rest of them" (p. 45). Later, Goggins explains to Chandra that "human
relations *are* largely play therapy anyhow. That set off an Indian
reverie: 'Who shall say how much play is earnest and how much
earnest is unwilling play'. . ." (p. 71). Unlike sexual and children's
games discharging aggression, the games of coercive society are

played in earnest, and engaging in play without understanding that one is playing involves a loss of an inhibiting perspective. The ex-Nazi, American scientist Dr. Untergang (probably a parody of Wernher Von Braun and Edward Teller) seriously argues before a United Nations gathering that "we should be stouthearted, and rather than risk the defeat of the Free World . . . gladly face the termination of history. . ." (p. 131). Before he has finished expressing such conventional Cold-War rhetoric, however, the delegates, motivated by Cocuficin, mob Untergang.

Authoritarianism is depicted by Goggins as having its origins partly in a sense of personal impotence, a viewpoint reminiscent of that of Braunstein in *No Such Liberty*. Goggins analyzes Dr. Cannon (a British physicist who, like Goggins, is asked to testify before the United Nations that testing nuclear weapons does not adversely affect human fertility in Asia). According to Goggins, Dr. Cannon is a "clever, overgrown schoolboy" having a "vast technical school inferiority complex, hell-bent on knighthood, who can be flattered into anything in consequence" (p. 38).

Like the inadequacies of the other power-loving personalities of *Come Out to Play*, however, Dr. Cannon's personal inadequacies have significant sexual dimensions. Described by Goggins as the "Chief bomb-maker," he has a name which patently combines phallic and artillery implications. His phallic-rocket obsession apparently functions to express aggression, domination, movements which simulate coital penetration, and orgasm (or potency). From an ethological perspective Dr. Cannon manifests low-dominance behavior. (A low-dominance person "is not confident in relationships with others" and feels compelled to assert himself "in what is an irrational way in order to be able to overcome anxieties."[36]) Coital play, like child's play, is a way of dealing with anxieties associated with dominance behavior. Consequently, Dr. Cannon's phallic-rocket obsession is dissipated as he discovers the ability to "grow backwards again in an adult context" (in the language of *The Joy of Sex*, p. 81), that is, the ability to come out and play. After he has become a student in Goggins's sex clinic, the perceptive Dulcinea informs Mrs. Cannon that her husband will "lose all interest in rockets the size of Nelson's column and bangs which" abolish "whole islands" if he once acquires proper sexual "control and a sense of confidence in himself. . ." (pp. 123–24). Dulcinea's prediction is fulfilled as Dr. Cannon is liberalized and humanized through Goggins's instructions. But Marcel discovers a less time-consuming antidote to authoritarian behavior. His general

aphrodisiac, 3-blindmycin, overcomes sexual inadequacies and dissi-
pates the interest of men and women in surrogate forms of power.

The view of sex underlying the conclusion of the novel may be
formulated in Freudian terms. Society represses the individual and
the individual's repression of himself is, in effect, repression by
society, for the authoritarian conscience, or superego, represents the
external authority or power of society internalized. The authoritarian
conscience helps to create irrational demands (Cold-War idealism,
for example). It also inhibits the individual's capacity to engage in
sexual activity as a form of play. Hence, the individual is unable to
transcend his sexual substitutes. 3-blindmycin dissolves the authoritarian conscience, as does, more slowly, the rational therapy
given in Goggins's clinic. And with authoritarian conscience dis-
solved, the individual is able to partially rediscover the repressed
potentialities of childhood and those of primitive, noncoercive
societies. Psychologically and mythologically, in other words, the
novel moves from Paradise Lost to Paradise Regained, from individual and social repression to individual and social liberation.

Like *Cities of the Plain, Come Out to Play* presents an explosive,
apocalyptic revolution in which power-centered society is destroyed,
but destroyed comically and nonviolently in a mushroom-shaped
cloud of pink smoke symbolizing sexual liberation. Towards the
conclusion of the novel Goggins watches in horror as Marcel, gone
mad, carries a quart of 3-blindmycin into Buckingham Palace. It is
enough, Goggins exclaims, to "liberalize the super-ego of every man,
woman and child on the earth's surface." To the incredulous Dulcinea, Goggins explains:

"You don't understand. You don't know the full significance of our institutions. Ten thousand years of humbug are like gravity. You tense your muscles
under it. This lot are shortly going to become weightless, and when the
British ruling class loses its inhibitions I'm not stopping by. Run for it—
everybody out of this lab:"
. . . .

Over the Palace, a pinkish mushroom cloud of vapour, covered with
suggestive convexities, was expanding slowly into the sun, like Venus out of
her shell. . . .

"There must be somewhere . . .," gasped Dulcinea, over the rising
clamour behind, "at the airport . . . darling . . . let's hurry."

A flock of pigeons in the road ahead stopped feeding and began to display to
each other.

"The *avalambitaka-bandha?*" I gasped back. I saw her true beauty for the first time, naked through her presentation clothes, running down the Mall.
"Anything, but be quick! So very quick!"
The uproar grew and spread and widened behind and around us. Holding hands, we ran on towards the Admiralty Arch. (pp. 220–21)

The utopian and political implications of *Come Out to Play* are similar to those of Huxley's *Island* which, reversing the pattern of Comfort's novel, begins with an Edenic utopia and ends with its elimination. In *Brave New World* Huxley had feared that nonrepressive sexuality might become unproductive displacement activity, siphoning off energy needed for social change. (As Comfort notes, Huxley was earlier "scared by the idea" of sexual liberation, but "came to become himself a Californian, and . . . ended up full of soma with a lady guru."[37]) An implication of *Come Out to Play* is that even liberals and radicals have nothing to fear from the new morality or the sexual revolution. Having lost most of his fears, Huxley in *Island* is similarly interested in Indian sexual techniques, in drugs to enhance sexuality, and in sexual liberalization as a means of liberalizing, and assuring the coherence of, society. Both *Island* and *Come Out to Play* also indicate that self-realization is to be achieved through the reconciliation of the Dionysian and the Apollonian elements of the personality, although the process of self-realization for Will Farnaby in *Island* has metaphysical implications that are foreign to Comfort's novel.

In its comic treatment of human sexuality, its humours characters, its puns, and clownish inclusion of asterisks (at the beginning of part four) as substitutions for bawdiness, *Come Out to Play* is reminiscent of the novels of Sterne and Fielding. Goggins is particularly interesting as the first of Comfort's protagonists manifesting a developed personality inasmuch as he possesses a full range of emotions and is capable of productive action in, or against, society. Comfort's earlier novels portray characters suffering from a loss of affective depth as the consequence of their roles as victims of an oppressive, asocial society.

With the exception of *The Almond Tree*, which focuses on protagonists becoming aware of death and meaninglessness, Comfort's novels are not conventional psychological novels. Nor does he create typical sociological novels, treating class or domestic conflicts, after the manner of eighteenth- and nineteenth-century fiction. Both internal conflict and conflict between individuals are minimized in Comfort's fiction generally. Rather, he emphasizes conflict between individuals and impersonal institutions. His novels analyze power structures. But the analysis, from the perspective of their narrative development, is usually not direct. Authoritarian institutions, like atomic particles in a physicist's cloud chamber, are generally examined indirectly through their effects: through images of rootless existence in an urbanized environment and descriptions of war and victimization in concentration-camp conditions.

To such indirect analysis Comfort adds the analysis of power structures provided by his victimized protagonists. Images of victimization and descriptions of protagonists struggling hopelessly with impersonal forces in *No Such Liberty, The Power House, On This Side Nothing,* and *A Giant's Strength* link Comfort's fiction with that of Kafka. But Kafka, by internalizing external authority, creates essentially psychological studies and, unlike Comfort, presents protagonists overwhelmed by an anxiety of guilt and freedom. Comfort's characters experience anxiety as the consequence of the remedial characteristics of modern society in which wars and political persecution threaten personal security and human existence. Moreover, Comfort's characters, unlike Kafka's, are portrayed as developing the rational capacity to pierce the confusing surface structure of reality in order to discern the causes and agents of their victimization. Images of mechanized existence in Comfort's fiction indicate that the realm of power is also the realm of death and the inorganic.

CHAPTER 4

Poetry

I   A Wreath for the Living

A *Wreath for the Living,* first published in 1942, includes eight of
the twelve poems of *France and Other Poems* (1941) and is itself
included in *The Song of Lazarus* (1945). According to Derek Stanford, it is with the publication of *A Wreath for the Living* that Comfort
first

attracted serious attention. Both in spirit and subject-matter the poems hit
the nail of the time on the head. The war poetry of a pacifist, they explored
more deeply the dark situation than that of any khaki poet with the exception
of Sidney Keyes. Unlike so many of the neo-Romantics, from the first
Comfort showed a strong grasp of reality. [1]

The poems included are often subjective in their obscurity and
surrealistic texture, but not autobiographical. Having little to
confess—Comfort is in his early twenties—and possessing no strong
sense of guilt over either private or public transgressions, Comfort
does not create confessional poetry, after the manner of Barker or
Thomas. Nor does he create, as do Hendry and Thomas, images
having psychoanalytic significance, dragging to light the destructive,
diseased forces of the soul.

The stylistic qualities and structure of Comfort's early poetry are
explicable on the basis of principles enunciated in "It Goes Like This"
(in *Life and Letters Today,* 1941). Comfort argues that "a coherence of
image" is

not antagonistic to the involuntary approach but necessary to it, if our work is
to be more than a catalogue of ravings. And we make our form by three
devices, unity of intention (not necessarily of the syntactical sense, but of the
source from which our images arise and the montage they produce)—word-

play with sound and assonance, use of rhyme and word similarity to cohere
our images, and use of a metrical form of some kind to make it move.[2]

His arguments concerning unity of intention recall Dylan Thomas's
explanation of his "dialectical method" operating within "imposed
formal limits": "a constant building up and breaking down of the
images that come out of the central seed. . . ." But less dialectical in
Thomas's sense, Comfort's imagery is less violent, congested, and
contradictory. The imagery of his early poetry recalls, more simply,
Fraser's definition of the "image" as used in Apocalyptic poetry.
Employing the cinematographic concept of montage to define the
"image," Fraser quotes from Raymond Spottiswoode's *Grammar of
the Film*:

Montage, he says, is "in its effectual aspect, the production of a concept or
sensation through the mutual impact of other concepts or sensations."[3]

Such a view of the image-making process invites ambiguous, symbolically suggestive imagery.
    "Waiting for the Wind" illustrates most of the stylistic qualities
catalogued by Comfort above. The poem alludes to the expected
German invasion of England, although its tone is apocalyptic, recalling Shelley's "Ode to the West Wind":

> The year turns—Summer blown from Europe
> fills skies with grazing islands, throws sickle beaches
> flecked with red feathers round uncharted bays
>
> only a day ago I saw a cloud
> grey as burnt straw, shaped like an ear of wheat
> lie tall across the country, from sky to sky
>
> preceding wind, a banner. Here in England
> how we lie silent watching the bowl of the sky
> how we lie silent waiting for the wind—

An impressive example of Comfort's theories concerning harness-
ing the "involuntary approach" by means of a "coherence of image"
is "The Atoll in the Mind" in which, according to Stephen Spender,
Comfort "works out the logic of a strange and beautiful image."[4] The
poem's ambiguous metaphoric structure is based upon the visual
resemblance between coral and brain tissue. The slow, unnoticed,

and hence corallike, evolutionary development of man's primitive, unconscious mind finds its complement in the late emergence of human consciousness and rationality. Upwardness and downwardness, lightness and darkness, and air and water help to suggest the fundamental dichotomy of mind and their union in nature, the desired synthesis:

> Out of what calms and pools the cool shell grows
> dumb teeth under clear waters, where no currents
> fracture the coral's porous horn
> grows up the mind's stone tree, the honeycomb,
> the plump brain-coral breaking the pool's mirror,
> the ebony antler, the cold sugared fan.
> All these strange trees stand downward through the water,
> the mind's grey candied points tend to the surface—
> the greater part is out of sight below:
>
> but when on the island's whaleback spring green blades
> new land on water wavers, birds bring seeds
> and tides plant slender trunks by the lagoon
>
> I see the image of the mind's two trees cast downward,
> one tilting leaves to catch the sun's bright pennies,
> one dark as water, its root among the bones.

In "Bird's Eye View of a Romantic Revival" Treece sees "The Atoll in the Mind" as an example of Comfort's "sensuous and long" lines which make "great and varied use of a liquid, musical language; using sound as an integral part of sense, and not as an exhibition in itself."[5]

Long lines, less sensuous, characterize the purposefully conversational style of "Letter from Safety," in which clock and slaughterhouse imagery imply mindless conformity and intimate death. Death is the price of such conformity, Comfort suggests, and, by means of a pun, compares the docile and dutiful citizens of the modern democracies with the war's horizontal dead:

> And yes, you are happy—even butchers' beasts
> must be alive to die, but not we upright
> clock-faced citizens, set to the same false time,
> all equal, all unanimous, waiting the signal to clap
> the conjuror's final swindle, strike together
> "How right we are, how right we are—" those chimes
> from the clock in the burnt-out house, the sole thing going
> when hearts have stopped and lives, but the clock goes on.

As in Thomas's "wagging clock" in "Especially When the October Wind," Time's "dial face" in Barker's "Epistle I," or Treece's "ticking dial" in "Selections from a Poem in Progress," clocks function elsewhere in Comfort's art as *memento mori*. Images of "clock-faces," while suggesting time's domination, primarily suggest the emotionless and mechanically obedient individuals who anonymously cooperate with or acquiesce in militarism and the status quo. The American anarchist Emma Goldman similarly indicated that the "highest attainment" of the state "is the reduction of men to clockwork."[6] Sheep or cattle, as in Wilfred Owen's "Anthem for Doomed Youth," in which Owen writes of "these who die as cattle," symbolize in Comfort's art the dehumanizing impersonality of war and the mindless obedience of citizens and soldiers.

Like "Letter from Safety," "The Bullocks" and "Carol for 1941" indict acquiescence in war's slaughter. "The Bullocks" confuses cattle-drivers with "mercenaries," or professional soldiers, and the journey of cattle to the abattoir with progress along the stations of the cross. It does so in order to show that soldiers and patriotic citizens who allow themselves to be sacrificed and emasculated (like bullocks) by government have reason to "envy these, fat beasts who die for food, / needing no speech to whiten out their dying. . . ."

"Carol for 1941" represents the Nativity story, finding in the baby Jesus a symbol for an indifferent, godless universe, and in both the crucified Christ and the traditional Nativity "ox" symbols for the perpetual sacrifices of war:

> Skew-crossed Orion leans to point the roof—
> a peach born out of season with no sun—
> the gold straws rustle under sightless God.
>
> Whom soldiers sing tonight under paper lanterns,
> where the drink is gold, and there are letters from home
> smelling of pine, fingered by far hands
>
> the perpetual son is born. The ox forgets
> under his cloud of meadow-smelling steam
> society which postulates his flesh.

Compared with other poems based on Christian myth and written at approximately the same time (such as Robert Lowell's "The Holy Innocents," Hendry's "Golgotha," Treece's "Christ Child," or Read's "Carol"), Comfort's "Carol for 1941" is not metaphysical, mystical, or sentimental. Nor is it a lament for the disappearance of innocence or a superior and meaningful tradition or culture. Comfort's use of secular myth, as in "Image of Venus" and "Hymns to Pan," is similarly devoid of wistfulness concerning the past and expresses the constancy of human experience.

"The Tyrants" is based on Comfort's view of two types of revolution: one, sexually repressive, rationalistic, and despotically equalitarian; the other, organic, subversive, richly imaginative, and not externally imposed. The poem also implies, through natural metaphors, the perennial and cyclical character of the struggle between Classicism and Romanticism, life and the forces of death and power. But image, not metaphoric meaning, dominates its simple, subdued stanzas:

> Coming by night the insurgent snow made equal
> hollow and ridge, blotted the stones, proscribed
> the party coats of trees, set upon leaf and pond
> its wise immaculate censorship.
>
> Under its unity all fields are level—
> wide streets are laid out in the pasture:
> the new rule purges the ways, flogs underground
> the harlotry, conscripts the hedgerow—
>
> presents an imposing front, on the slopes not broken:
> hangs medals on the grasses, does not hear
> the rank sedition steaming under—
> the pent seed, the twig randy for springtime.
>
> Thinking of the thin globes on Christmas trees—
> green, red, imp-haunted, infinitely fragile—
> the children walk through the white woods in mittens.

Skeletal imagery appears frequently in Comfort's early poetry. The preoccupation of the Apocalyptic poets with such imagery is probably of significance to Comfort's art. Treece, whom Comfort particularly admired, employs skulls and bones, as *memento mori*, in "The Shapes of Truth," "Martyr," "To the Edge and Back," "Pilgrim," "Invitation and Warning," "The Poet," "The Varied Faces," "Speech for Hamlet," "Elegy Unending," "Legend," "See-Saw on Dying," "I Locked Love's Door," "Betrayal," "Captured Moment," and a number of other poems. Treece is particularly obsessed with the word "bone," but frequent images of corpses, graves, and tombs also appear in his poetry. Comfort's imagery is generally less gothic. *Memento mori* images of "bones" appear frequently in Hendry's poetry, as well as images of geese gabbling in "skeleton jigsaw" in "Europe: 1939," a "cross-ribbed Adam" (Christ) in "Golgotha"; a "skeleton" and "cloud-skull strangling sky" in "Apocalypse"; and a "chilled skull and spine" and "bone-shriek-splinters" in "Picasso—For Guernica." Like Hendry in "Conversation with My Heart," Comfort presents images of singing bones and ships of ribs. Skeletal imagery in Comfort's poetry, furthermore, sometimes takes on a sexual suggestiveness reminiscent of the employment of such imagery in the poetry of Dylan Thomas.

José María de Heredia's lovely "Le Récif de Corail" may have motivated Comfort's "The Atoll in the Mind." Comfort's sonnet entitled "From the French of Heredia" is apparently modelled after Heredia's "Le Naufrage." Some of Comfort's alterations are made to unify his poem around the *memento mori* image of a ship of ribs. In "Le Naufrage,"

> Avec la brise en poupe et par un ciel serein,
> Voyant le Phare fuir à travers la mâture,
> Il est parti d'Egypte au lever de l'Arcture,
> Fier de sa nef rapide aux flancs doublés d'airain. . . .
>
> O Terre, ô Mer, pitié pour son ombre anxieuse!
> Et sur la rive hellène où sont venus ses os,
> Soyez-lui, toi, légère, et toi, silencieuse.

In "From the French of Heredia,"

> He sailed from Egypt with the dogstar rising,
> sailed with a following wind and a clear sky,
> twin skins of metal on his quick ship's ribs—
> seeing the notable lighthouse cross his rigging. . . .
>
> Sand, drift him softly, wash him quietly water,
> having regard to his much-travelled spirit,
> and his ribs scattered on this classical shore.

"Elegy on a Hill" is reminiscent of an Anglo-Saxon riddle. The opening lines present a deathly image of a bone resting in a groove made by a "crack in the boulders" (st. 9) of a hill. In this uncovered grave the bone "sings" its history (st. 2–9), and is also said to sing because it is whistling in the wind (cf. st. 9). The moss and lichen spread over it, or largely disappear, according to the season:

> And now the bone sings in the dark furrow
> and the pulses of moss go over it season and season
> the lichens' tides, and the feet of the wild ponies
> treading dark water under the dark hill—

Simultaneously the imagery of these lines is sexual, the movement of male and female parts in line one, and the pulsating movement of ejaculation in the following lines.

In the following stanzas sexuality and procreation are intimately connected with death, as in the poetry of Thomas. The bone while inhabiting its former body, its phallic shaft the man's "lever," had received from the procreative act "sons of a brown girl in winter," children inescapably fated for death in the season of death. The inescapable prescence of the bone, or skeleton, in the child and man suggests the Thomasesque moral. Death permeates life. The forces of physical as well as psychological disintegration develop simultaneously with physical growth and mental development.

The sexual act and procreation provide for the "man" and his wife a momentary triumph over death (st. 5–7). But their victory is illusory. The grey mosses have covered the porous outer layer of the bone (the "grey mosses have marched by all my pores"). And the bone now waits "for the sky," waits for the flesh to be gradually removed by natural decay, the rain and the wind, and the beaks of birds ("the wind my midwife, the beak and the rain's fingers," stanza nine):

> "The ponies rush and scatter the ribs my brothers,
> and the grey mosses have marched by all my pores—
> For I am master of him who never saw me
> while under his skin I waited for the sky.
>
> "He lay two moons by the dripping crack in the boulders
> the wind my midwife, the beak and the rain's fingers.
> So I was born and washed and the third day christened.
> But when my wife came by, she did not know me. . . ."

Commenting on the last two lines, Derek Stanford argues that "the poem concludes with a laugh against the bone, which is not, after all, a substitute for the total personality."[7] The primary implications of the concluding lines, however, seem to reinforce the poet's moral concerning the final triumph of death. "Elegy on a Hill" is vaguely suggestive of the death by crucifixion of Christ on a hill called Golgotha, "that is to say, the place of a skull" (Matthew 27:33). The ironic concluding lines allude to the triumphant affirmation of St. Paul: "that Christ died for our sins . . . and that he was buried; and that he hath been raised on the third day. . ." (I Corinthians 15:3–4). But this by contrast is a resurrection to eternal death.

"Elegy for a Girl Dead in an Air-Raid" recalls Yeats's "Death" and Rilke's "Die Vierte Elegie" in its depiction of man's tragic capacity to comprehend and anticipate death. As in Rilke, lions are examples of natural beings lacking a sense of futurity:

> And still below the stars the mind's quick eye
> opened in error weeps to see its end:
> for the stones see nothing, the lion the past only,
> and does not know the bones beneath his hide.

The poem is also in some respects similar to Thomas's "Refusal to Mourn the Death, by Fire, of a Child in London." The concluding phrase of Comfort's elegy, "Death without end" (Part VII, st. 4), is reminiscent of Thomas's elegy in both language and meaning. Moreover, this elegy, like Thomas's, laments the death of an anonymous child caught in the tragedy of war who represents all the nameless and often innocent persons who have died and are dying because of the war. The adoration given to the dead girl, and her identification with the Virgin Mary, establishes the girl as the apotheosis of Comfort's humanistic religion of solidarity and responsibility in a world torn by war:

> Lady, under this tree I kiss your hands
> knowing your tree to be the Spanish olive
> for you and I remember the sun on metal
> and fifteen bodies scattered across a road. . . .

Comfort's phraseology and choice of images, his reference to a lady under a tree, to her white appearance, to the Virgin Mary, and to skulls and bones, invite comparison with Eliot's *Ash-Wednesday* (Part II). But whereas Eliot's lady is associated with Ezekiel's resurrected bones, and is also a reminder of the awful separation of the Divine from the human, Comfort's lady is a manifestation of the poet's sanctification of ephemeral human life in a godless world. The concluding stanza contains an allusion to the twenty-third Psalm which undercuts any conventional religious meaning which might be attached to the elegy by reminding the reader of the inauthenticity of all who seek to escape from a realization of death as personal extinction:

> grant you who feared no evil find no heaven
> being happier so: puffed out by history
> with every good and every beautiful flame
> before you learned this forest. Death without end.

The concluding line ironically alludes to the "Gloria Patri": "As it was in the beginning, is now, and ever shall be. World without end."

"The Orioles," written "For Stefan Zweig," departs from the usual format of Comfort's elegies to the extent that it is about definite individuals. It is an effective statement of Comfort's compassionate response to the news of Zweig's death. Stefan Zweig and his wife are the orioles. Zweig, in exile in Brazil, suffered from increasingly acute depression over being unable to return home (the Gestapo, he explains in his letters, had auctioned off all of his property) and over his growing conviction that the war in Europe would take years to complete. He committed suicide, with his wife, on February 23, 1942. Comfort's reference, in stanza one, to "your wise hands" ironically and ambiguously refers to Zweig's hands as a writer, but hands that took his own life. The poem gains in complexity through Comfort's later depictions of Zweig as a "surgeon"; Europe (st. 3) and England (st. 4) are portrayed as dying patients whose fatal disease is discerned by Zweig:

> Asking myself how long yet, whether the end
> was in sight, I heard you dead.
> Gone both together, you and your wife, two minds
> outside the gate of Europe. Your wise hands
> went out to find a childhood you remembered.
>
> It is true that the beautiful die and only they.
> Because its wings are strange, we kill the oriole
> a simple stranger coming once in a life.
> So the plumed mind means death. . . .

Comfort's reference to Lazarus (st. 4) is to both the Lazarus whom Christ raised from the dead, and consequently ironically symbolizes a

resurrection to life that Zweig will never know, as well as to the
biblical beggar Lazarus, who died to find eternal rest in Abraham's
bosom. The reference to the latter Lazarus indicates that the sense of
human solidarity, evident in Zweig's compassionate life and writings,
is the only solace that those who realize their mortality shall ever
know: "I think of Lazarus—/foresee no bosom for you, but your lamp/
your pity being Abraham in our minds. . . ."

II Elegies

Elegies, published separately in 1944 and included in *The Song of
Lazarus,* contains a series of eight elegies as well as a poetic epigraph,
"The Syracusan Expedition," and a concluding poem, "Epitaph."
Like Gray's famous elegy and Anglo-Saxon elegies such as "The
Ruin," these elegies do not lament the death of an individual, but
rather the frailty and transience of human life in general.

"The Syracusan Expedition" established the immediate context in
which the elegies are to be read. It links the young soldiers of World
War II, "our first born" (st. 3), with the first-born slain by God as He
traveled through the land of Egypt at midnight (the "moving shadow"
of death in stanza one). The "following tide" (st. 1), a reference to the
bloodstained trail left by the Deity, intimates as well the subsequent
deaths of Egyptian soldiers in the Red Sea. The "Egyptian cry" (st. 1)
refers to the "great cry" which rang throughout Egypt at the time of
the slaying of the first-born (the last plague):

> Now that the edge of darkness finds our coast
> and some are confident, and shake their fists
> at the moving shadow, at the following tide
> and the Egyptian cry will rise tonight
>
> I cannot think of chaos as it was—
> I saw the flowers, not the skull that fed them:
> imagined rivers in a summer country
> wash the cold evil from the land we knew.
> But what we shall bury with our firstborn now
> is not corruption only, nor virtue, but mankind. . . .

Comfort's allusion to the Egyptian dead, with whom is buried the
"corruption" of Pharaoh's enslavement of the Jews, indicates that his
compassion for soldiers who are dying is intermixed with his pacifist
rejection of the cause for which they fight. Egypt here is associated

with authoritarianism and militarism (as in Comfort's *Into Egypt*, a play).

The fact that England is an island like Sicily and that London is under siege (the blitzkrieg) as was ancient Syracuse by the Athenians in 415 B.C. provide for Comfort basic points of comparison. The allusion to the Syracusan expedition indicates that democratic England will probably repel her German invaders, but may not be the same politically afterwards. A period of democracy preceded the Athenian invasion of Syracuse. Although successfully repelled, the invasion was followed by a return to tyranny in Syracuse and the rest of Sicily.[8]

The remainder of the poem establishes the larger philosophical context in which the elegies are to be read. It is essentially a reassertion of Comfort's conclusions concerning the emergence of a pervasive awareness of death in a meaningless universe which are developed in *Art and Social Responsibility*. In both works Unamuno is used as an example of the artist who expresses or reveals the fundamental elements of the modern death-oriented "Zeitgeist":

> How will they stand, the hand on plough and wheel
> naked seeing it—that which the kindly hid,
> Unamuno and Rilke walked with it,
> ingeminating daily in the blood?
>
> For now as children opening the locked room
> innocent come on unforgettable death
> or seeking pictures in the topmost book
> uncover knowledge that makes end of life
>
> the time is short, till each of us suddenly,
> singly by night, or marching, winner, loser
> come upon purposeless Infinity.

In the "First Elegy" the Freudian (as well as Classical and religious) symbol of death as a journey is intermixed with images of doomed vegetal and animal life:

> Perpetual death, that falls on the single leaf
> perpetual darkness, end of flower and thought
> perennial country, where we are going, whither
> all winds blow, all lives tend, all leaves fall,
> to the blind attic full of broken faces
> under the cold and heavy muzzle of the years.

Stanford sees the image of "the blind attic full of broken faces" as a "typical *Wasteland* figure" which describes here the "traveler's final bourne" and which "recalls the cellar with the 'rats feet over broken glass'—just such another hutch of moral values; a shack in the dust-bowl of the mind's history."[9] The image, however, suggests the rather conventional final repository of family photographs which are "broken" or cracked with age (as well as, perhaps, covered with glass that has also been broken). That this attic is "blind" implies, perhaps, that the dead, like their ageing photographs, are neglected and rather quickly forgotten by the living. It implies primarily, however, that this attic allows no exits and involves "perpetual darkness."

While having in common with Eliot's imagery in *The Waste Land* a suggestiveness of both death and meaninglessness (but more precisely here, death as meaningless), it is highly unlikely that Comfort's image of our "final bourne" resembles in other respects Eliot's images of contemporary sordidness and moral decay. Comfort's "blind attic" to which "all lives tend" is another illustration that "the lesson of all living is death" (1. 9). The concluding lines of Part One show that "this truth" makes continued enjoyment of life difficult. Comfort's view of death in Part One is close to that Unamuno, who argued that the concrete individual "finds life insupportable if death is the annihilation of the personal consciousness. . . ."[10]

In the "Second Elegy," Part One, Comfort develops an ingenious metaphysical conceit. In the opening stanza the troubled sea over which the "seasons" flow "like unquiet winds" reminds the poet of his own inwardly troubled existence and of the seasons or ages of man:

> Hearing the sea troubled, across its furrows
> an eagle song, and down its moving lanes
> the seasons flowing like unquiet winds—
> the transit of sea-pebbles in the dark

The following stanzas reflect the theory that all life comes from the sea, and that, in a sense, man still carries the sea within him.

The saline composition of the blood may have been determined by the saline composition of ancient sea water. It is here, consequently, the "captured sea that goes with us," a "darkened ocean in my skull," with its "imprisoned salt" as a "captured arm of sea," and its "salt levels dark as oil" (st. 2 and 5). The moon measures time here in the cyclic movement of flood time followed by ebb time in the poem's external and internal seas (st. 2–5). Darkness intimates death and the lightless condition of blood within the body. The blood, like the sea of stanza one, is unceasingly moving, flowing through the wheellike orbit of the circulatory system, measuring the restless ages of man until its circulation ceases in death (st. 5). Seeing further resemblances in things apparently unlike, Comfort describes the skull knitted together by the cranial sutures as the "jointed ceiling" which "creaks" and echoes hollowly the movement of the blood, like a cave lapped by the sea (st. 3). The "sunless waves" of the blood break on the "channelled bone" of the skull as well as on the "devious honeycomb and crack" of the cerebrum (st. 2–4). And without footprints left on the fleshy white beaches of the brain (st. 4), the dark flood of blood ebbs and flows:

> we hear the captured sea that goes with us.
> I know a darkened ocean in my skull
> the same moon drawing its tides in the sea's reins
> the sunless waves breaking on channelled bone
>
> or sleeping, its salt levels dark as oil
> reflect no clouds. The jointed ceiling creaks
> and the cave's drum repeats the blood going.
> There swim no islands and no freckled fish
> only by devious honeycomb and crack
> on the white printless edge of level bays
> lick the incessant ripples, black like sleep.
>
> The imprisoned salt, this captured arm of sea
> turns my unquiet seasons in its wheel
> till it flows back, behind a falling tide.

Such an interpretation does not preclude other possibilities. It seems likely that Comfort's description of a darkened internal world owes something to the descriptions in Classical literature of the darkened and gloomy underground world of Hades in which the Stygian lake (or river), across which Charon ferries the dead, functions as a symbol of death.

In Part Two of the "Second Elegy" the fear which accompanies the recognition of life's brevity and precariousness is symbolized by "the charioteer riding upon the mind" in stanza two. The "polished snake" which sheds its skin suggests the possibility of transformation or metamorphosis: i.e., an interruption or reversal of the process of ageing that could "check" its "headlongness." But such taunting possibilities cannot apply to the poet who pictures himself as left

holding the snake's wrinkled and unregenerate skin, a haunting
reminder of the gradual and irreversible wrinkling and deterioration
which the process of ageing involves:

> no rise and fall of hills, no peaceable stone
> can check the headlongness—the polished snake
>
> leaves in my hand his unregenerate skin.

The imagery above is also sexual, intimating, among other things,
that a diminished libido, or ineffective phallus, is also associated in
the poet's mind with ageing and death.

In Part Three of the "Second Elegy" Comfort again presents
images which link death and sexuality. In stanza one "flowers" and
"buds" (and perhaps "houses" as well if we follow Freud in viewing
houses as symbols for the human body) rather overtly retain their
sexual significance as well as their significance as symbols of the
transience of human existence. In the following stanzas the image of
the fishlike plow points to the interruption of agrarian life by the
transformation of peaceful peasants into murderers in war (an inver-
sion of the biblical transformation of swords into plowshares):

> The year flies on and darkness gathers now
> over the small house and the single field. . . .
>
> the plow's bright fin that hungers in the field
> ripples at evening on a pool of blood;
> sorrow is cold. . . .

The images (above) also connote sexual activity, sexual energy that
here has been converted from its function of procreation and as a
manifestation of love into the destructiveness of war. The concluding
stanzas similarly treat the frustration of love by the war's separation of
young lovers and the despairing sublimation of human energy (including sexual energy) in the thanatotic activity of the war in Europe:

> Now when the night wind covers the hills, I know
> so many thighs empty as children's yearning
> flame-like across the coasts
>
> to where twin enemies seek the breasts of the soil—
> under the night's white hawthorn, milky with sorrow
> sleep out their hours.

In the "Third Elegy" red apples dropped from the apple tree symbolize human fragility, decay, and death (st. 1). The "Shadows of birds and their small bright mouths" provide an ominous forecast for the fate of the apples. The presumably rosy "faces of children" are likened to the "reddening globes" of the apples, and the birds of death, like the squadrons of fishes that tatter the dead face in the "First Elegy," wait to pick the flesh of the fallen apples. Images of birds, and in the "First Elegy" of fishes, tearing flesh are reminders of the hostility or indifference of the universe, and recall the observations of Tennyson's tormented narrator in Maud: the "Mayfly is torn by the swallow . . . And the whole little wood where I sit is a world of plunder and prey." However, the emphasis in Comfort's poetry is not on interspecies hostility, or on the fact that life is required to live at the expense of life. His birds and fishes are portrayed devouring dead flesh rather than preying upon other forms of life. Comfort is suggesting the pitilessness of natural processes rather than reviving or reemphasizing a Darwinian view of life pitted against life in a mad struggle for the survival of the fittest.

More than other political philosophies, anarchism is a peasant philosophy. The "Fourth Elegy" alludes to the peasant refugees who fled or are still fleeing the occupying or contending armies in Europe:

> And still the winds of Europe blow in my mind
> I have seen the endless faces, the faces of friends
> crossing dry plains under the swinging hills
> the carts moving—the women's terrified faces
> the carts moving under an empty sky.
>
> Always since childhood I have seen my friends—
> Europe like a dark sky, dotted with sheep
> and the fires of forges, made by the smith and the shepherd.
> Now the moon lights the anvil on the shoulder,
> the night wind ruffles a thousand stumbling fleeces.

That the "Fourth Elegy" treats perennial peasant types (the "smith" and the "shepherd") partially explains why Stanford's comment on this elegy is as ambiguous as the elegy itself. According to Stanford, Comfort "identifies himself with a continent of sorrow and with those previous centuries of grief that have helped to fashion his present cast of mind."[11] What is of importance is the recognition that Comfort is referring to the refugees of war. His use of perennial peasant types, besides indicating that element of society with which he identifies, tends to generalize his depiction of war-torn Europe. That is, Comfort's depictions of the victims of the Second World War apply equally well (or better) to the victims of previous European wars, and are consequently a reminder of the never-ending tragedy of war.

The "Fifth Elegy" contrasts children playing and old men on park benches showered by leaves. The tragic condition of the old men holds the center of attention. Their "pink open lips" and the dropping seeds (st. 1) simultaneously connote both new life (human and vegetative) and decay (ageing) leading to death, as does also, more explicitly, the image of their closed hands with palms "furrowed as children's" (st. 2). The old men watch (st. 4) and wait (st. 7) and wonder whether the future contains any further springtime possibilities or only the signal of death, the "dull horn," sounding in winter, followed by a death-room pillow and finally a tombstone (contained in the image of the pillow like snow-covered landscape which winter skies darken into the appearance of stone):

> whether the clouds will graze again, and the limes flower—
> the swallows' faces brush at the window-panes—
> whether the gardens will open to their slow steps;
> or the dull horn blow, later, in colder days,
> the pillow's landscape darken into stone.

The "Sixth Elegy" has as its geological focus a harbor area and seaport town (st. 1), and probably does not describe "a visit to a lonely fishing island," as Stanford remarks:[12] The "island" referred to as "Ireland's Eye" is apparently in the "blind bay" upon which the seaport town is situated (st. 2). (That the poet is not on the island, but looking at it, is indicated also by his later references to the "immortal island" which "watches with brown eyes" (st. 18), the "brown eyes" being the "walls on a brown flank" referred to in the second stanza.) Stones, pebbles, rocks, coral, shells, and fossils intimate here, as well as elsewhere in Comfort's early poetry, the transformation of the living organism into its static mineral state, the hostility of nature, and the security and permanence of inanimate nature in contrast to the insecurity and transience of human life. As in the poetry of Fraser, Treece, and Thomas, the changing seasons are, once again, conventionally connected with ageing and death (st. 9).

Less conventional in meaning is the image of the mysterious stranger which the poet meets while walking on the beach. Stanford believes that the "poet narrates an experience which recalls its

counterpart in *Little Gidding*, where T. S. Eliot describes how he
meets the image of his ancestor face to face."[13] The mysterious
stranger here is silent rather than didactic and informative, but the
situations of both poems are somewhat analogous. Comfort's mysterious stranger is clearly a *memento mori*. The poet faces the fact of
personal as well as universal death by recognizing his deathly double
who carries the message of death, and who is likened to a macabre
Pied Piper leading a procession of the dead:

> It is most strange walking to have met myself
> between the sand and the water, half in sunlight
> a mindless figure on the yellow beach
> its hands idle, walking to carry a message—
>
> and from its feet ran back the winding prints
> into the sea. . . .
>
> Passing each other we had nothing to say,
> but the dead followed him under the dunes, a circle of
>   lipless faces
> as children follow music, lagging but following,
> fish in a sea of grass. . . .
>
>   The sailing island . . .
> sent up myself to meet me in the sunlight
>
> the piper whom below the grass
> follow the unwilling dead, disposses children. . . .

The "First Elegy" invites the reader to "learn" from natural
symbols "how death-in-living labours in our bones." That lesson, the
theme of all the elegies, becomes particularly prominent again in the
eighth and last elegy of the series, and is expressed by means of a
parable. The poem begins in typical parabolic fashion ("There was a
woman in Asia. . . .") and recounts the story of a woman who was
buried while bound to a corpse. The corpse's algae-covered belly
rubbing against her "open rose" in necrophilic simulation of the
sexual act heightens the hideousness of the woman's condition, and
ours (st. 2–5). The literal as well as thematic conclusion of the poem is:
"Look down today and see your bedfellow" (st. 17 and 6). Such an
attitude towards the process of ageing as it leads towards death is
similar to that of Yeats in "Sailing to Byzantium," in which the poet is

"sick with desire and fastened to a dying animal." But in the "Eighth Elegy" there is no surrogate paradise in the world of art to provide a compensation for the loss of personal identity in death. The "Epitaph" which follows again presents osseous imagery to remind us of death, and, like the epigraphic "Syracusan Expedition," gives to the elegies a political direction: "the shoreward dead are friends to all/at whose heels yell the clock-faced citizens."

"Aeschines in Samos," appearing both in *Elegies* and *The Song of Lazarus*, contains, as Stanford observes, an image of "an old man" which "serves to recall the Gerontion of Eliot and parts of his 'Song for Simeon' as well."[14] The old man is Aeschines Socraticus, the ancient Greek rhetorician and the poem's narrator, who finds that rhetoric is no match for death and the silence of the grave:

> The Aegean has no rhetoric
> licking the pumice round this skeleton island
>
> where the rocks are hollow and the springs are hot
> and all the waves run back an unreal blue. . . .
>
> The fear of childhood is not exorcized
> the sea, the unimaginable darkness
>
> upon whose edge I sit. . . .
>
> Tonight I shall not sleep, but I shall recall
> the juror's faces, the crowd's wonderful roar. . . .
>
> I will consider what you say. O Argas
> washed by the sea, my friend, I have no rhetoric
>
> an old man sitting by the edge of darkness. . . .

Aeschines's reference to "Argas the banker," who "was a friend of mine," but has drowned while "sailing off Athos," is intentionally specific; for Aeschines scornfully calls Demosthenes, his enemy, "Argas" in his speech "On the Embassy" (343 B.C.).

III   *"The Song of Lazarus"*

"The Song of Lazarus" appears both at the conclusion of *The Song of Lazarus* and towards the conclusion of *The Signal to Engage* (1946). The poem is dedicated to Paul Eluard and expresses the sort of sympathy for suffering humanity and anger against the perpetrators of injustices that characterize much of Eluard's poetry. Like Eluard in "Charniers," "A L'Echelle Humaine," and "Les Vendeurs D'Indulgence," Comfort castigates the "whistling butchers" (Eluard's "les bourreaux") who do not remember the war's "voiceless" dead, the "Argus eyes/of the voiceless" (Part Eight).

Abstract concepts appear in "The Song of Lazarus" and in a number of the poems of *The Signal to Engage* and *And All But He Departed* (1951) in a manner reminiscent of the use of abstractions in Neoclassical verse, but point towards an opposite conclusion. The abstract concepts of social morality, Comfort's poetry indicates, have no absolute, transcendental existence and are as artificial and illusory as the sense of relatedness which conformity to such morality provides. The antipathy of the Apocalyptic writers towards abstractions probably exerted some influence upon Comfort's thinking, as did the attitude towards abstractions evident in much anarchist thought. Kropotkin stated the anarchist position:

We refuse to assume a right which moralists have always taken upon themselves to claim, that of mutilating the individual in the name of some ideal. We do not recognize this right at all, for ourselves or anyone else. [15]

Abstract morality transmuted into the catchwords and slogans of war propaganda is Comfort's primary concern. His poetry, in this respect, recalls Roy Fuller's "Spring 1942," in which is drawn a distinction between the imposing, idealistic slogans of propaganda and the concrete reality of personal death. In Fuller's poem a chaplain speaks to a group of soldiers:

> "Freedom," he said, and "Good" and "Duty."
> We stared as though a savage spoke.
> And we made no reply to that
> Obscure, remote communication. . . .
> O death, our future;
> O revolution in the whole
> Of human use of man and nature.

In "The Song of Lazarus," Lazarus speaks of having "lain grovelling under the bombs of the Bringers of Freedom. . ." (Part One), and the poet, addressing his son in Part Four, unmasks the insidious tricks of the propagandists who justify war as a means of gaining or maintaining freedom:

Remember when you hear them beginning to say Freedom
Look carefully—see who it is that they want you to butcher.

Remember, when you say that old trick would not have
    fooled you for a moment
That every time it is the trick which seems new.

IV   The Signal to Engage

The polemical tone and relatively plain style of "The Song of
Lazarus" link it with the poetry of *The Signal to Engage* in which, as
Stanford observes, Comfort eschews " 'fine writing,' " his verse now
becoming "even more direct with its cogency and vivid homely
logic."[16] "Song for John Hewetson" laments the imprisonment of
Hewetson, one of three anarchists connected with the Freedom
Press who were imprisoned for sedition in 1945. Hewetson's arrest
for sedition came shortly after a government raid, on the twelfth of
December, 1945, against the Freedom Press. That raid prompted a
formal protest (printed in *The New Statesman and Nation,* March 3,
1945) against "the increasing tendency in England . . . towards the
restriction of the liberties of statement and persuasion."[17] The protest was signed by Alex Comfort, T. S. Eliot, E. M. Forster, Ethel
Mannin, John Middleton Murry, Herbert Read, Reginald Reynolds,
D. S. Savage, Stephen Spender, and Julian Symons. The following
year Comfort in *Freedom* reviewed Hewetson's *Ill-Health, Poverty
and the State,* praising Hewetson's highly documented study of the
relationship between capitalism and the ill-health of the poor.[18] The
imprisonment of Hewetson (both physican and libertarian
sociologist, like Comfort himself) is for Comfort in the "Song for John
Hewetson" evidence of the topsy-tuvy character of asocial society.
Finding a resemblance between prisons and coral, also cellular,
Comfort protests against a system in which political reformers are
imprisoned by criminals:

Only the single light which each life keeps,
the fire of disobedience, lies awake

and the dark head of coral, packed with men
glows like a round lamp in the darkening sea
grows till it breaks the back of some foul ship

and spills to drown its crew of murderers.

"None But My Foe to Be My Guide" is partly about the unconscious destructiveness and purposelessness of the physical universe.
The beauty and "faultless order" of the stars in the opening stanza
tauntingly intimate a moral structure to a benign universe. But their
incredible distance from man make the stars convenient symbols for
the indifference of the universe as well. Stanza three describes the
forlorn condition of modern, Romantic man whose values are as
perishable as man himself and intimates the meaning of the title of the
poem; for the Romantic's adversaries—a universe inimical to life and
human values and power-centered personalities and institutions
which curtail human freedom—define his philosophical stance:

> For us who fight now, there are no signatures—
> no kings or godheads set their names on leaves
> Beauty like us has a more perilous life,
> and Freedom is not written on the stars—

The political focus of the poem is indicated in the opening stanza in
which references to prisoners provide political connotations to the
term "neutrality," connotations which are extended to stanza four in
which the reader is informed that "the stars did nothing" for anarchist
political prisoners, such as Nicola "Sacco." In a war-infested country
become a "butcher's field washed in the tides of words [propaganda]
and hunger," such modern Romantic rebels are "sentries at the
wood's edge" who stand

> and see the people a cloud that moves and gathers
>
> bearing its dark yeast, headless, moving, afloat,
> mustering unhurried against the wind of the time,
> til a great anvil stands across the sky
> and under the moving cliff the fields fall one by one
>   silent
>
> until amazing, a blue, elbowed stream,
> suddenly flies like light tyrannicide,
> dazzling, making a noiseless pause, and then
> in its track crashes the rain upon hills that give back
> echoing bank by bank the flat cheers of thunder.

The vision is apocalyptic. The cloud, affected by the wind of time and
molded by its own inner principle of change, "its dark yeast,"

assumes the shape of a "great anvil"—a symbolic expression of a movement significantly peasant and proletarian in character—from which springs lightninglike sparks and the sound of thunder like the deep metalic roar of hammering. Both spark and thunderbolt, the "elbowed stream" flies like an avenger, strikes down tyrants, purges society.

In the biblical Apocalypse the fiery destruction of the powers of this world is followed by the resurrection of the saints, the triumphant shouts of the heavenly multitude, and the establishment of the messianic kingdom. Comfort's poem echoes that pattern:

> Though they have taken so much, we still remain—
> we have brought lamps into a lightless cave,
> and in the end we are makers of new things.
> And all these voices under the light soil
>
> are seeds, and there will spring a flowing crop
> laid level now, like waves in a long calm
> wherever they have plowed. And every seed
> for the pause falling between thunder and rain
>
> waits now. There will rise then a sea, spring then a
>   voice
> that will outtop the heads of Citizens, and its noise
> at that cloud's hem clinging we listen for.

The elements of the apocalyptic vision of "Sunday on Hampstead Heath," by the anarchist George Woodcock, are similar:

> And here where my friends talk and the green leaves
>   spurt . . .
> I see a world will rise more lovely than Blake
> Knew in his winged dreams, and the leaves of good
> Will burst on branches dead from winter's hurt.
> When the broken rise and the silent voices speak.

The concluding stanzas of Comfort's poem, echoing meanings established earlier, indicate that the individual's sense of identity and meaning in a meaningless universe is defined by his perpetual antagonists:

> For Freedom and Beauty are not fixed stars,
> but cut by man only from his own flesh,

but lit by man, only for his own sojourn
because our shout into the cup of sky
brings back no echo, brings back no echo ever:
because man's mind lives as his stature's length

Because the stars have for us no earnest of winning
because there is no resurrection
because all things are against us, we are ourselves.

It is in man's hopeless struggle for ideals that will ultimately perish with man that such ideals become truly vindicated: it is the unheralded struggle to the death of the "endless millions" in stanza four which gives reality to the ideal, for "they died to give this thing a name." Moreover, "None But My Foe to Be My Guide," as well as much of Comfort's poetry generally, implies that there is a sense in which the impermanence of human values and of human life and their uniqueness in a meaningless universe make both values and life not less valuable, or of no value, but more valuable.

Comfort's view of nature, expressed in "None But My Foe to Be My Guide" and a number of his other early poems, is distinguishable from that of other Romantic and neo-Romantic writers who, while depicting nature's terrifying destructiveness, often intimate some utlimately meaningful underlying reality. Treece drifts towards a sort of elemental Wordsworthianism, asserting in "Pastoral," "I have learnt nothing from the marble urn/The sparrow could not teach me."

"The Postures of Love," a poem in five parts, represents an enlargement of "Three Love Poems" in *The Song of Lazarus*. The poem imitates Thomas's "Light Breaks Where No Sun Shines" in celebrating love, sexuality, and procreation in ambiguously symbolic images that intimate that life and the ecstasy of love are relentlessly permeated by the knowledge of death. Comfort also follows Freud by regarding the erotic instinct as more or less identical with the life force or will to live. Part One represents a world in which death seems to be excluded and in which nature is in apparent harmony with human life. The woman which the poet sees in "a green field" is a kind of earth mother representing sexuality, procreation, and life. Her song celebrates life and the imagery suggests her essentially sexual and procreative nature. From her breasts daisies drop like milk (st. 2) and milky flowers move in the upright wind which her song has created (st. 4). The "field of ears" (suggestive of the receptivity of

nature to her song) and her "bright beads" suggest (in a description
which recalls the "river" brought down by her "song's long finger" in
stanza five) phallus, semen, and copulation in the concluding stanzas:

> there sang a woman in a field of ears
> and her song like bright beads scattered
> fell round her thighs among the grass
> for this song is living, is time—
> no virgin knows this song but women only

As in Part One of the "Postures of Love," our attention is largely
focused upon the poet's description of a woman in Part Two. However, the poet here is not interested in celebrating the procreative
powers of a woman, but in celebrating male sexual potency. In "The
Lovers," one of the poems of *A Wreath for the Living*, horses
represent the forces of sexual passion erupting beneath a deceptively
placid exterior. Here the "white mare," which represents the lady of
the poet's reverie, has similar symbolic implications. More explicitly
sexual is the image of the "open rose" surrounded by "dark hair" (st.
3). The meadow landscape of stanza one anticipates the landscape
imagery of stanza three, which also represents female physiognomy.
The sea covering the pebbles in the following and last stanza repeats
the image of stanza two and prepares the way for the ambiguous,
copulatory image of the poet riding the crests of the waves—the
subdual of the "unridden" white mare of stanza one: "her pebbles
lying under the dappled sea./And I will ride her thighs' white
horses." As in Part One, the poet has again described an exuberant
world in which the forces of life are triumphant, apparently. The
whiteness of the mare here carries its conventional associations:
virginity and innocence. But the association of whiteness with death
later in Part Five has retroactive implications. Moreover, the rose
and sea, associated with life in Part Two, are symbols for ephemerality and death as well; in Part Five the sea is clearly associated with
death.

Part Five formerly followed Part Two in "Three Love Poems." Part
Three of the "Postures of Love" was originally the concluding poem of
"Three Love Poems." Its theme, that love is inescapably ended by
death, is still the logical conclusion of the new five-part poem. The
phrase "closer than the grave's/white tangled dancers"—that is, the
skeletons of lovers who have been buried together—has been added
in stanza two in order to emphasize such a conclusion, as well as to

bring the poem (Part Three) into closer harmony with the subject suggested by the new title. The opening stanza of Part Three is about the hostility or indifference of nature. The stars move across the indifferent or "stony" heavens like a school of fishes, and the "star's white mouths" are a "net of mouths" in which life is entrapped. The movement of the stars, like the movement of the moon in Part Five, is itself a *memento mori*; it is time, traditionally measured by the movement of celestial bodies, which consumes. In the last half of Part Three the movement of the hungry lion around Christian lovers condemned to die reminds the poet of the movement of the stars (with perhaps a suggestion of the constellation Leo in the reference to "the lion").

In Part Four the "postures of love," as in Carew's "A Rapture," are interpreted literally, anticipating Comfort's interest in sexual techniques in *Come Out to Play, The Koka Shastra, The Joy of Sex,* and *Haste to the Wedding.* In stanza one Briseis, the slave and mistress of Achilles, her "master," is a bridge to be spanned, and her thighs ("her wheeling waves") are breaking against his phallic "rock." In stanza two the crowd that came to watch the race between victorious Milanion and Atalanta has gone home. Atalanta in turn achieves some victory over the supine Milanion (1. 7), but it is Milanion who achieves the victory necklace (1. 8).[19] Helen's way with Menelaus after the fall of Troy is the kneeling position of the penitent, facing away. The way of Octavia, the wife of Mark Antony, is more conventional; her white body moving in copulation ("her white horse galloping beside his own") recalls Comfort's description of the "white mare" in Part Two. The way of Lais, the notorious Greek courtesan, is, appropriately, that of an "outspread ship," ships being symbols for the female body, according to Freud. The "swimmer on her whitening pool" is perhaps the philosopher Aristippus (one of Lais's suitors) who, according to Athenaeus, compares Lais to a ship in which many have happily sailed.[20] The life-force, or Eros, temporarily gains the ascendency over the forces of death in Part Four, and, as in "Elegy on a Hill," sexual activity has temporarily provided an escape from the consciousness of death. But that such an escape is only temporary is emphasized by means of the reference to "the clocks" in the concluding stanza.

The copulatory theme of the "Postures of Love" is continued in its fifth and final part, although more obscurely. The emphasis on the passing of time—"the clocks"—at the end of Part Four is continued in the image of time passing in the crescent moon growing into the full moon in the first stanza of Part Five, while simultaneously semen, womb, and orgasm are suggested. The landscape symbolism of Part Two is also revived. The woman here is a "field" to be plowed; her sexual organ is represented by "furrows" and "hollows," and her soft but firm breasts are represented by "mountains/stranger than feathers, hard as fishes." The male principle here is represented by "rain" which makes fertile the "crops." Water and whiteness intimate death and the inextricable connection between death and sexuality. The white body of the narrator's fair mistress is now a "white continent" (presumably virgin territory, now newly explored) "on all whose beaches break the seas of years/this is the surf they say the dying hear."

The moon's light casts a romantic aura around the lovers in stanza one of Part Five; hence, their "bodies grow blue like pebbles in a stream." But the imagery is simultaneously cadaverous. The "watery cloth"—a continuation of the image of the "net of waters" of Part Two—suggests a death shroud as well as lover's sheet, and the marble, frozen bodies, grown blue, are suggestive of corpses as well as satisfied lovers.

"The Postures of Love" contains elements of conventional Renaissance love poetry which are ironically modified by the poet's dark, Romantic obsession with the destructiveness of death: specifically, his celebration of his sexual prowess and his mistress's fairness and physical charms, his representation of feminine innocence preparatory to courtship, his depiction of his mistress as a continent to be explored, his sympathetic references to Lais and other figures of classical mythology, and his vision of love's constancy. The culmination of the sexual act bears enough resemblance to physical dying to have caused the metaphysical poets of the seventeenth century to write of orgasm as dying, and that meaning is not excluded from the various parts of Comfort's poem. But it is consciousness of time which here transforms the sexual act into a meditation upon death. From the lifeless, moving sea of time there is no rest or escape—there "no rock rests the gull, and no tree stands/ever . . ." (st. 4). The sexual act itself, simultaneously, heightens the poet's awareness of death, as in Robert Graves's "Pure Death."

V   And All But He Departed

Less rhetoric and Freudian symbolism and a tighter logical, syntactical, and narrative structure characterize the poetry of *And All But He Departed* (1951). The subject matter is varied, but the preoccupations of Comfort's earlier poetry continue. "Anacreon's Grave" explores the mind of Anacreon, whose lyric poems, such as "Woman's Arms," "To His Young Mistress," and "The Picture," celebrate the physical charms of his young mistresses and his own enduring sexual abilities. Comfort presents Anacreon in his extreme old age, his wrinkled body a grave for his former self. But age, physiological age, is relative, and Anacreon, who can still "sing/and whore" despite his "apple-shrunken face," is not as old as his former mistresses, whom he perceives in their ruin. In "And All But He Departed" the poet and a friend, while walking to Strandhill, scare "the docile sheep" with protest songs "that scared governors." Seeing their shadows "On the mist" as "big as a hill side," the poet thinks of the departed anarchists, such as "mild Sacco," which their songs celebrate. The concluding reference to "Prisoner and conscript" waiting "Until the turn of the times/Brings England's Easter week . . ." presages a resurrection of the aspirations of departed anarchists, a political or social revolution. "The Petrified Forest" treats the deterioration of an ancient civilization through the failure of its members to "disobey," distinguishing between genuine moral responsibility and the conformist's false sense of duty. "A Virtual Image" is reminiscent of the "Sixth Elegy" in its use of the poet's double, now his "mirror shadow" with "feet set to an unattainable sky," as a *memento mori.* "It Is Expedient That One Man Die for the People" constitutes an argument against the sacrifice of life for life and the conventional morality which rationalizes war; the poet reverses the assumptions made by biblical writers (as in John 11:50). Society's perennial, irrational, and destructive deification of its abstract ideals and moral principles is the subject of "The Tribal Deities." Its title recalls Comfort's parody in *Authority and Delinquency* of the bankrupt prescription of the "traditionalist reactionaries and 'back-to-nature' revolutionists" for the ailments of twentieth-century man: "While there is time, let him turn back; let him abandon science and revert to common sense, the tribal deities, and the past" (p. 107). The "deities" of "Belshazzar and the Wall" (st. 3), also tribal, are employed by the ancient tyrant and, by implication, his modern counterparts, to rationalize violence and economic exploitation. Like Belshazzar's kingdom, modern power-centered society is weighed in the balances and found wanting and doomed. "The Mermaid" distinguishes between the unseen self and its external masks, the body and what Jung called the "persona." The title of the poem refers to the unseen self of the woman addressed by the poet, a self that is beautiful, but elusive and hidden, like a mermaid. The poet, in Paris and separated from his mistress, concludes, "I know you better when I cannot see you:/touching you makes you further." "Seeing the News Films, January, 1951" displays arresting imagery and irony and eloquently speaks for the innocent victims of war (the Korean War in particular):

> One turned her back. A Child carried a child.
> A child ran searching, will always run. No sound
> out of his desperate oval mouth—what we have written
> we have written: nothing will change it. If
> we shout *Look, she is there he will not hear*. . . .
>   You stay with us
> an after-image of the colder light
> on a white ground, dark—on the white ground
> dark, beside the path, a liberated child.
>
> And I the child will run always, but never knowing
> a senile general and ten frightened men
> for whose prestige I, suddenly lost,
> being four years old, and seeming
> after long searching to have fallen asleep
> am here, cannot be buried. In this immutable dream.
> Once we could kill people and they would die.

"Children in the Luxembourg Gardens" has as its subject the inescapability of death. The poem, which records the poet's reactions to a "Picture from an Exhibition," the subtitle, begins with the poet's interpretation of the painting and describes children playing in a world in which death appears to have no part, the static and timeless world of art. It is also a world, like that which Yeats envisions at the conclusion of "Among School Children," of aesthetic pattern, balance and harmony:

> The park of children is a point in time—
> chestnuts and fountains in a mild september
> stop in the warm light as a picture stops
> in time. One cannot tell
> which is the fountain, which the tree.

The painted fountain, "moving always," yet keeping "its air/of constancy," parallels in the poet's imagination the painted tree which like all actual trees combines apparent stillness with movement: "and one more still/cloaks with its leisure the fine leap/from seed to foliage up." By the end of stanza two, however, the tone of the poem has darkened and become more complex. The image of the children racing in play beneath the tree—"a flicker of children under the fountain of leaves/whose posture runs more quickly than their feet"—contains in it something suggestive of the ephemerality of childhood. And the image of the "Old men" who "like mushrooms ring their cards and skittles" provides a faint intimation of mortality in this world of "mild september."

In the final stanzas of "Children in the Luxembourg Gardens" the sense of death's inescapability becomes increasingly more pronounced. The poet first addresses a "fellow student" who has suffered from one of the improbable accidents of warfare, or from an enemy soldier with exceptionally good aim. Comfort's pun suggests both possibilities: "You, fellow student, hit by a long shot/of this last war. . . ." The tree, a symbol for natural generation in stanza two, now is associated with death, and its "fountain of leaves" now becomes a "hail of leaves"—suggesting the hail of bullets in battle—which have "blurred" the "old fighters" in the painting. The following image of the "wheel of green to metal turning" (st. 3, 1. 4) suggests the cyclical transformation of green summer to rust-colored autumn in this "mild september." It also echoes the sense of the previous line, the "hail of leaves"[21] that are reminiscent of the hail of bullets in warfare; the "bark" of the tree "joins lips over" the bullets shot during the wars. The fountain, associated in stanza two with children and lovers, continues that association in stanzas three and four. But Comfort's characteristic association of water with death, as well as the color white with death, shapes the macabre meaning of the fountain as another locus, like the tree, which, while suggesting the forces of life, masks tragedy and death:

> Children's fingers
> after one summer will not find the place
> where in the wood's white water a child lies
> or from the fountain bowl a child's face answers
> their faces in the crinkled glass.
>
> It is perhaps your mouth the lovers kiss
> your tricolor spectrum flies at the fountain's peak.

The child's spectrum, or afterimage, is a reminder—like the traces of war left in the trees of the park—that death is inescapable and permeates life. It is towards the same conclusion that we are driven

by viewing the "tricolor spectrum" as meaning a flag patterned after
the flag of France; for it is the dead child's flag which has supremacy
here.

"Concerning the Nature of Things" begins with a description of the
battle of Thermopylae and an allusion to the Trojan War in order to
explore the unending tragedy of human mutability. It concludes with
the poet's affirmation of an atheistic and materialistic point of view
which removes the fear of death:

> I lie
> at peace with matter, myself
> being material
> and holding in my hands all justice that there is
>
> and fear gone out like smoke
> and the sun chasing the fear
>
> even of the dreamless night.

Such conclusions echo those given by Lucretius in *De Rerum Natura*
to which Comfort's title alludes. Lucretius's atomistic materialism
forms the basis of his rejection of the notion of immortality and its
attendant rewards and punishments. Death disperses the unbreak-
able atoms of the body and brain, Lucretius teaches in the second
book of his philosophical poem. In the middle of Comfort's poem, the
poet solves the riddle of life and death:

> Midday in the island is
> the sand of a green pool
>
> the sun falls in a shaft
> from a knothole in the door
>
> the smoke of a fire runs
> in a fold of wind, dust
>
> yellow like small bees
> is swarming without a sound
>
> moving its gold net
> dust is the key to it
>
> multiform dusts, a sufficient answer.

But whereas Lucretius teaches that the universe has no center, Comfort finds that the universe has a "center" inasmuch as all things move towards physical dissolution (a variation of the implications to be derived from the second law of thermodynamics):

> In the fulness of time: all things
> move to a centre, travel
>
> by mile or inch, to reach
> the effortless still Sargasso sea—
>
> the smooth shot of water, the sharp
> anchors of metal, the soft
>
> globes of oil, the dull
> burrs of earth move
>
> unbreakable ductile dusts
> the motes in the knothole beam
>
> being what they are, travel
> like bees at sundown back.

Comfort's image of the Sargasso sea recalls that of Thomas's "When Once the Twilight Locks No Longer."

VI   Haste to the Wedding

Haste to the Wedding (1962), Comfort's latest volume of poetry, was found, as Drasdo observed, "disappointing or distasteful in some quarters."[22] Imposing conventional moral judgments, Anthony Thwaite, in a review for *Encounter,* characterized Comfort's poetry as "sniggering jollity" and "high-class dirt with lots of fashionable literary references." Thwaite concluded that Comfort, "who wrote a handful of moving sensual love poems in the early 1940's seems to have degenerated into middle-aged prurience."[23] More sensibly, Donald Davie in *New Statesman* wrote that Comfort recommends "animal aplomb" with "elegance, impropriety and wit." Davie argued that Comfort is as "resourceful" as Robert Graves (Graves's *New Poems* appeared the same year), although Comfort "leaves out a lot more; his is a very stylized world indeed."[24] Davie's measured appreciation is appropriate. The poems of *Haste to the Wedding* bear many of the characteristics of the *New Lines* poetry of the so-called

"Movement." Lucidity, accessibility, rhyme, and structured form now characterize Comfort's poetry. The theories of Freud, the poetry of Thomas, and Christian phraseology and myth, all influences upon the style of Comfort's early poetry, are now subjects for witty analysis. The Freudian explanation of the creative impetus, a problem for Read and the Apocalyptic writers, is treated in "Sublimation" and "Another, on the same." In "Sublimation," the poet concludes,

> The songs that stand are sung
> chiefly by hungry men.
> With better things in hand
> no one would dip a pen:
>
> the written word provides
> a form of exercise—
> the gist of poetry
> you have between your thighs.

Pun and *double entendre,* as the lines above indicate, are very much a part of Comfort's style in *Haste to the Wedding.* A *double entendre* in "Another, on the same" allows the poem to begin and end with the word that Judge Woolsey found acceptable for Joyce.

"Dylan Thomas on a gramophone record" wryly treats the sort of vicarious immortality at which Hardy scoffed. The "mortal moon" has "struck a druid blow,/and her sickle has reaped Dai Barleycord/as clean as mistletoe. . . ." Now metamorphosed into a gramophone record, Dylan is "fixed in his grave and corkscrew groove" and, like the crucified Christ, "waits the resurrection." But Dylan's mechanical resurrection—"holding the thorn against its breast/the wafer turns to word"—provides no vicarious immortality, for he is "starched bodiless out of the reach of love" and "the word that lies in that black host/can never again be flesh."

"Sacred and Profane," "After you, Madame," and "The Young Nuns" treat what Comfort in *Sex and Society* refers to as the exploitation by Christianity of "sexual anxiety," an exploitation which is a "source of its authority" or power (p. 64). "Sacred and Profane," the atmosphere of which resembles Davie's "The Evangelist," provides an attack on one of the favorite doctrines of institutionalized Christianity, the superiority and durability of the "Love of the Soul" to physical passion. Spiritual love is as deadly as the robe of Nessus given to Hercules by the jealous Deianira; physical passion is less dangerous and demanding:

Love of the Soul is Deianira's robe:
soul loves are adhesive, greedy, cannibal—
rape is their natural mode. Bodies, more genial,
ask less—give more. No violence
matches the Jack-the-Rippers of the soul—

The final stanza inverts conventional Christian expectations, consigning the practitioners of spiritual love rather than carnal lust to hell fire.

"After you, Madam," ". . . is like a melody," "In the Museum," "Never say Never," and "A Social Contract" are love poems in the Classical and Neoclassical traditions. Like "The Postures of Love" (Part Four), "After you, Madam" celebrates sexual diversity. The human capacity of such diversity, not the Western belief that some nonfrontal positions are animalistic, is taken as evidence for man's superiority over his animal ancestors. The poem also provides criticism of role fixations of the male-chauvinist variety. "Adam," the mythological expression of a patriarchal society, provides the model for male exploitation and impersonalization of women. Punning, Comfort also finds that "casuists of the Vatican" appear to take *"au pied de la lettre"* St. Paul's recommendation that women should submit themselves to—be under—men. Such theology is a "source of *mauvaise honte"* over diversity in sexual behavior. Petronius, the master of Nero's revels, "knew better" because he knew less:

There are no upper hands in love
though one is under, one above:
            the man who said so lied—
it is a choice for human mates
lacking in other vertebrates
            that you or I should ride.

Adam, that Freudian figurehead,
considered his prestige in bed—
            taking their cue from that
the Moslem schoolmen who believe
in the delinquency of Eve
            extend her like a mat:

The casuists of the Vatican
in placing woman under man
            take Paul *au pied de la lettre.*
Before the mediaeval *conte*

> made it a source of *mauvaise honte*
> Petronius knew better.

Playful humor and a measure of metaphysical wit characterize "A Social Contract," which in its subject matter (his mistress's bosom) recalls the poetic preoccupations of Robert Herrick:

> —*Fanno baruffa:* today your twins
> have quarrelled again and turned their backs.
> Next week they'll be childish, reconciled
> but still born unequal—the left one
> (called Jean-Jacques Rousseau) always takes precedence.
>
> Pious unbalance of an Islamic rug
> that must not tempt perfection, but tempts me—
> each month they rise and fall, like slow breathing—
> ensure that the first sight I ever saw
> won't pall, but be my uplift till Death weans me:
>
> each keeps its own *haeceitas* through change,
> my noble savages. . . .

"The Young Nuns" is about chastity as a religious ideal. The nuns, "never alone," nevertheless live lonely and sterile lives. The authoritarian structure to which they belong is likened to a bee-hive society, and from each "falls constantly" the unproductive, "honeyless buzz of prayer."

"At the Exhibition of Mexican Art" links power-centered societies, both ancient and modern, with death:

> This stone fiend is the God of Government,
> Coatlicue, the Skull Venerable.
> Goddess of napalm and the United Nations.
>
> We know there were societies of death—
> chaste, warlike, cruel: military louts
> victorious chiefly over women and prisoners
> bending the customs of a milder people
> to clubs and slaughter-stones and engraved tables
> of laws beginning "thou shalt not," ending "shall die."

The poem expresses the Kropotkinian conclusion that the mores or customs of life-centered societies were sufficient to guarantee social order and cohesion. But the transformation of such societies into societies based on coercion involved the selective codification of those mores which were most likely to reinforce the principle of coercive authority.

"The Stranger's Gallery" indicates that modern democracies may be only superficially humane, and ultimately more dangerous than the monarchies they have supplanted. Now lawyers and politicians, more straitlaced and businesslike but less individually powerful, ape the authority of the old absolute rulers:

> After the Sultan dies, the monkeys come
> benignly scratching in the ruined court-room—
> more dignified, in fact, than he had been:
> less formidable, lacking his opportunities.

The image of "Mister Pontius Paradise"[25] connects pompous bureaucrats, the false political paradise of modern democracy, and the first-century prefect who represented Roman imperial power in Israel. Like ancient Rome, modern democracies are imperialistic and tyrannical. But they are also administered by thanatotic bureaucrats addicted to Cold-War rhetoric, power, and racism:

> We have pulled out the teeth of Government.
> where once it sat, there is the jawless face
> of Mister Pontius Paradise
> and all the other jawless faces
> democracy propped to a sitting posture—
>
> remarking now and then, a mule's falsetto:
> "If necessary, we will end the world."
>
> Long-lived, short-sighted, plausible, insincere,
> pompous—and spiteful on a minor scale
> they are not tyrants to the unpigmented
> they bully only that which will not bite
> raw prefects of a rather nasty school.

"Maturity," placed at the conclusion of *Haste to the Wedding*, castigates idealists turned middle-aged reactionaries. Fear and the bribes and temptations of materialistic society—Browning's explanation of Wordsworth—help to explain the behavior of those who turn to the state communism of "Uncle Joe," Catholicism, or Eastern Mysticism[26]:

> Let them turn to the bottle
> the Yogi and the rope
> some of them go to Uncle Joe,
> some of them to the Pope—
>
> one by one grown prosperous
> of excellent intent
> they set their names on the payroll
> of God and Government;
>
> one is turned evangelist,
> another is turned Knight:
> let them go wherever they wish—
> we will stay and fight. . . .
>
> All fierce beasts grow corpulent,
> mature and come to hand.
> Lions lie down with sheepskin wolves—
> we will see them damned.

The rhythms of the chants and protest songs of England's pacifist demonstrations of the 1950s and early 1960s animate the pugnacious stanzas of "Maturity." Qualities of humor, satire, bawdiness, chattiness, and generally nonmetaphoric prosaicness associate some of the poetry of *Haste to the Wedding* with that of the English Augustan period. But Comfort's philosophical assumptions are unfalteringly Romantic and libertarian. Poems such as "A Fair Exchange" and "Circe, and others" present rational alternatives to socially conditioned responses to adultery. Under attack in "A Fair Exchange" are conventional attitudes towards women as property and the so-called double standard. The poem's narrator, cuckolded, observes,

> You "had" my wife, you say—as if you'd had
> Lockjaw or pups: cheer up—I'm not the Moor.
> "Behind my back":—you mean "in privacy":
> You'd hardly put up posters. . . .

"Circe, and others," which improves on Waller's rebuttal to jealousy in "A Plea for Promiscuity," wittily depicts Ulysses explaining to an emotionally and intellectually mature Penelope

> how a strange woman bound him unawares,
> and so left-turn off the main road of love

> jolting across the fields into her private lane—
> and fed him there to all her succubine fancies,
> unholy but delight—
> and that abduction is his alibi.
> They were all you, he'll say, each one was you.
> If he is many-counselled, she is the wise—
> she'll answer "Show me," and believe it so.

A preoccupation with the establishment of rational attitudes towards sexual behavior and with the emancipation of women, as in the works of Emma Goldman and Mary Wollstonecraft Godwin, is fundamental to anarchist and libertarian thought.

The general drift of Comfort's development as a poet, like that of Thomas and Treece, is from obscurity towards clarity. Death and power are his preoccupations as a poet, but in *Haste to the Wedding*, as in *Come Out to Play*, are partially transmuted into their opposites. Rather than focusing predominantly on human impotence, despair, death, and external, institutionalized power, Comfort celebrates the individual, particularly his sexual abilities, and joyously affirms life rather than death.

CHAPTER 5

Conclusion

INASMUCH as organic unity is dependent upon dominating themes, as DeWitt Parker argues in *The Analysis of Art* (1926), the formal, organic unity of Comfort's artistic productions may be said to rest usually on his emphasis on man's struggle against the forces of death and power. In Comfort's works, moreover, the themes of death and power are interrelated and find in his continuing interest in human sexuality their counterpoint and, in many ways, their antithesis. The struggle against death and power in Comfort's work is, in Freudian mythological terminology, partly the struggle of Eros against forces productive of biological and social disintegration.

Thematic analysis of works of art—pursuing the artist's use of one or more themes—functions synthetically: I have been concerned with both the thematic unity of individual literary works as well as with the interconnections between Comfort's works generally. Thematic analysis generally functions on the simple and common-sense assumption that works of art are produced by individuals who are themselves organically structured. As current terminology would have it, personality, although continuously being modified, should be perceived as a gestalt. Art, from such a perspective, can never be said to be an escape from personality. It may represent a masking of personality or an attempt to minimize subjectivity through impersonal subject matter or modes of expression: for example, through impersonal, photographic realism. With respect to the latter possibility, where the artist sets his camera is of significance. The Zolaesque naturalism of *The Power House* is radically different in technique from the lyrical, subjective verse of *The Song of Lazarus*. But what is being recorded in the novel says as much about Comfort's continuing preoccupations (moral, political, and psychological) as anything in his early poetry.

Besides approaching Comfort's works thematically, I have, more generally, relied throughout this study on the methods of logical and descriptive analysis. Logical analysis is also synthetic inasmuch as it allows the critic to analyze a work of art into its component parts in order to reveal more completely the relationship of parts to parts within an interrelated whole. In this sense it finds its analogue in the biochemical analysis of living matter: of a cell, for example. In descriptive analysis the critic's own presuppositions may be held in check in order to allow a phenomenological approach—the critic views the work of art as its creator views it, so to speak.

A distinction exists between literary criticism based on descriptive and logical analysis or evaluation (as in chemical evaluations) and criticism intended to provide hierarchical appraisals of literary works and their authors. Such a distinction parallels that between so-called "descriptive" and "prescriptive" grammar and between purely descriptive and analytical judgments in sociology, psychology, and anthropology and normative or ethical value judgments about human behavior. Such conclusions are not to be understood as implying that normative judgments are not of extreme importance to human beings as human beings. A problem with normative judgments is not that they are unimportant, but that they depend upon unprovable philosophical assumptions usually colored, or largely determined, by unconscious biases.

A major problem with normative judgments is that artistic works possess no intrinsic value but only assume value in reference to human needs. Human aesthetic needs have some constancy, but wide variability depending upon cultural conditioning and, possibly as Comfort has argued, innate variability. In "On Laying Plato's Ghost" (in *Darwin and the Naked Lady*) Comfort writes:

Science has . . . nothing to say about intellectual "absolutes" (though it may have a great deal to say about values, if they are intelligibly defined). It has a certain amount to say about divergencies in taste which is important to criticism. . . .
Medicine is currently acquiring from biology the idea of human polymorphism. This means that there may be not, as we once assumed, one kind of digestion which is "normal," but a number of kinds, discontinuously distributed. . . .
The significance of this in medicine and psychiatry is obvious, but contrary to appearance it has also a bearing on one of the pretensions—and functions—of aesthetic criticism. It is not very upsetting to criticism that a tone-deaf man cannot enjoy music, even if tone-deafness is heritable. Those of us who are not tonedeaf can condole with him and go on listening. But what

about the suggestion that there is a true polymorphism in taste,—not in the quality or the intensity of the taster's experience, but in appreciation of a given kind or school or manner in art?

Tastes in Balinese or Akan art differ internally very little by our standards—the range of tastes in our society, like the range of beliefs, personality-types and standards, is a true polymorphism—chiefly of the epigenetic or sunburned variety, but, no doubt, with some strictly genetic traits involved, . . . Our society is a mixture, as it were, of the consequences of every upbringing from Samoan to Aztec. We have already seen how this diversity affects sexual behaviour—its effect on artistic behaviour is the same, and so to a large extent is the underlying mechanism. Thus tastes not only differ, they may differ irrevocably, and certain tastes correlate so closely with other personality traits as to be predictable. . . .

The defence against nihilism here is not an absolute standard—(the chief thing that aesthetics, like ethics, can learn from science and the consequences of science is that abandonment of the absolute for the empirical does not produce moral disaster)—but the fact I stated earlier in a far less provocative context—that the human aesthetic sense, like the human moral sense, is an adaptation which generates another adaptation. Darwinism applies with suitable modifications to art. I am suggesting that our criticism should be Darwinian. (pp. 123–28)

In light of such considerations it is appropriate that my own evaluations of the relative significance of Comfort's art and literary career are confined, essentially, to this concluding chapter. Some statements and evaluations appearing in this chapter, however, should be understood as implying philosophical presuppositions about the function and character of art. Such presuppositions may be analyzed but never proved (or logically demonstrated) to everyone's satisfaction.

Since this study has dwelt at some length with the relationship between Comfort's art and nonliterary works, an indication of the relative merit of his nonliterary works seems in order. *Art and Social Responsibility* is to be recommended as the best primer available for readers interested in understanding the conceptual basis of Comfort's literary works of the 1940s. In itself it is of significance as probably the most theoretically developed manifesto of the neo-Romantic movement. Of all his nonliterary works (with the exception of his pioneering studies in gerontology), *Sex in Society* and, more particularly, *Darwin and the Naked Lady* and *Nature and Human Nature*, represent his finest achievements both stylistically and intellectually. The long quotation above from "On Laying Plato's Ghost" suggests the high degree of perceptiveness and originality characteristic of *Darwin and the Naked Lady* and *Nature and Human Nature*. *The Joy of Sex* deserves recognition as the only Western manual on sexual techniques which measures up to the standards of *The Kama Sutra*. But it is a humorous work and written in a highly informal, racy style for popular consumption.

With respect to the quality of Comfort's thought generally, he is probably the most intellectually gifted, as well as the most educated, of the neo-Romantic writers of the 1940s and after. Herbert Read manifests comparable intellectual abilities. But sociologically and, more generally, scientifically, Comfort is more competent than Read. He adeptly approaches human experience in his later works through his extensive study of animal and human biology, as evident in *Nature and Human Nature* and *Darwin and the Naked Lady*. The provocative insights on the nature of art appearing in *Darwin and the Naked Lady* grow out of the fortuitous fusion of his biological and artistic interests.

Comfort's finest literary achievements are his lyrical, elegiac, and late love and satirical poems. Nevertheless, his novels have been generally underrated as compared with the recognition given to the merits of the poetry. Because the novel is a more conceptual, less symbolic, mode of organizing experience, Comfort's novels, which present or imply subversive conclusions, predictably elicited a greater degree of hostility (or indifference) from reviewers. With the exception of *No Such Liberty*, his apprentice novel, they manifest a kind of tough-minded yet sensitive approach to their subject matter that raises them above most popular fiction. *No Such Liberty*, *The Power House*, and *On This Side Nothing* are developed and conclude realistically, avoiding the conventional tragic atmosphere and conclusions of much Romantic literature as well as wish-fulfilling, shallowly optimistic implications. On a moral level his novels indicate that rebellion is an unending process, that neither total defeat nor total victory is in the offing.

Comfort's most durable achievements as a novelist are probably *The Power House* and *On This Side Nothing*. Both works manifest the sort of descriptive vividness, emotional intensity and depth, and unity in variety, or harmonious organic form, which we normally associate with major works of art. The fine organic unity of *The Power House*, Comfort's most generally complex, internally varied, and skillfully constructed novel, is based largely in his use of the image. Subsidiary imagery supports two dominant images which function as the balanced center of the whole: i.e., the images of the power house and the slaughterhouse. These two images are, in turn, reflections of each other. The power house (particularly as the symbolic image becomes interpreted more broadly in parts four and five as signifying the war machine) is a slaughterhouse. The slaughterhouse at which Fougueux works contains its own sinister engine, a power house in miniature, and emblemizes the emergence of a European slaughterhouse of war.

The aesthetic structure of *The Power House* has this in common with that of Comfort's early poetry: both employ the *montage* as a basic unifying device and as a means of interpreting reality. The reader is impressed with the stark reality of industrialized existence in France in *The Power House* through images, not discursive analysis. No analysis of its images in isolation from the *montage* in which they are anchored will fully do justice to Comfort's technique in the novel. Merleau-Ponty correctly views a film as "not a sum total of images but a temporal gestalt," and observes that the "meaning of a shot . . . depends on what precedes it in the movie, and this succession of scenes creates a new reality which is not merely the sum of its parts."[1] The novel is developed cinematographically and, according to Comfort,[2] key selections were written for the screen.

The Power House explores personality from the outside in by describing behavior shaped by environment rather than by focusing on the self-reflecting ego. Again, the technique is cinematographic, although it may be described as well as a modification of Zola's naturalistic approach to character. Character development in the novel is in the direction of modifying environment and behavior by modifying the relationship between behavior and environment: consequently, it is inescapably a novel of social protest. Rather than resting in the position that man is the inevitable victim of external forces over which he has no control (naturalistic pessimism), *The Power House* shows that the necessary interrelationship between behavior and environment is the basis of optimism. Environment can be altered.

Like other neo-Romantics Comfort writes in reaction against the pretentiously intellectualized style of Eliot and Pound. But his poems are usually more complex then those of the major Apocalyptic writers, Treece, Hendry, and Fraser. They are distinguished by complexity of three sorts: Classical allusions (generally unnoticed by his critics, as in the case of "Aeschines in Samos"); political and philosophical implications (also often unnoticed or misunderstood);

and verbal complexity: puns and irony in *Haste to the Wedding,* obscure and ambiguous symbolism in the early poetry. Biblical, topical, and geographical allusions also occasionally complicate some of his poetry. In "Cellar—(Balham, 1940)," for example, the poet, in Balham, a district of London two to three miles from the Thames, describes human faces, silent, illuminated by the flickering lights of war and shelter conditions:

These faces—the cold apples in a loft
huddled in rows—each shining green
catching a convex light, under the grey rat's foot
impotent, are not so quiet—

grey faces, hollow where the wasps
have been at them, after the fungus—turnip lanterns
are not so empty, impartial between self
and the small house under the imminent thunder.

These do not vary as the mind flickers,
blue hollows under jaws, shadows on throats,
not knowing, lying as apples lie
listening to the rat coming through the paper.

Only in this quiet, this hot listening, we hear
the hiss of stars in the river, going out.

Where Comfort's poetry is surrealistic in texture, its form is often more spacial than temporal. "The Atoll in the Mind" succeeds partly by communicating a sense of what Comfort in *Nature and Human Nature* refers to as " 'dream time' " (p. 168). Its narrative development, as I have suggested earlier, implies something about the evolutionary process. But its ambiguous figures move outside of time, because timeless, and are called Dionysus and Apollo. The form of "The Postures of Love," in which motifs and images reverberate and undergo metamorphosis, has about it a similarly successful development of spacial form, its rhythm lying not so much in its metrics as in its repetition of images in various stages of transmutation. Dream-time imagery allows, or necessitates, ambiguity of meaning, in Comfort's poetry a relatively high level of ambiguously symbolic complexity.

The preoccupations of his poetry are the preoccupations of his novels in much the same way that the preoccupations of dreams, it is often assumed by behaviorists, are the preoccupations of waking life.

There is not, I think, much "disguising," in a Freudian sense, of repressed wishes. His iconoclastic rejection of the demands of the superego (the conscience of the collective) would, it could be assumed, make "disguising" unnecessary. Where the latent content of Comfort's art is disguised, as in *Cities of the Plain*, there is evidence that Comfort consciously transmuted the heterodox content of his art into symbols (such as an erupting mountain signifying revolution) that were ambiguous enough to disallow his being trapped by the objective disciplinary force of the collective superego.

The moral function of literary art is not, on a practical level, separable from its aesthetic function. But morality must not be defined too narrowly. (Gide's *The Immoralist* has its own negative moral function to provide in its perceptive distinctions between conventional morality and the impulses of amoral human nature.) Morever, works of art should not be evaluated from the perspective of some crystalized, systematized moral or political ideology. The propagandistic attacks on Comfort's art and thought, in the light of such considerations, are not justifiable. There is nothing fundamentally immoral about his art or thought. Where his art suffers it does so from an excess of morality, an extravagant concern that the moral import of his writings will not be ignored by the majority of his readers.

The moral achievement of Comfort's art is not that he or his personae or protagonists argue successfully for anarchist alternatives to asocial institutions. Rather, it is that his art calls the reader back to the elemental fount of morality. Comfort's works treat the possibilities as well as the existential limits inherent in the human condition and the necessity to transcend doctrinal, racial, and national differences through an attitude of responsible concern for the poor and the weak. In this sense the particular solutions he advances are of less significance than his general moral orientation. Critics with axes to grind or reactionary views, such as Orwell and Anthony Thwaite, have reacted clumsily to Comfort's radical views. Orwell, in effect, found Comfort too Christlike, too willing to turn the other cheek. Thwaite found a later Comfort writing "high-class dirt" and having "degenerated into middle-age prurience." Neither view is to be recommended. Comfort's art is an art of protest, and where it does not convert, it provides, nevertheless, the valuable function of challenging and unsettling the reader's ingrained, comforting beliefs—hence, one reason for the unusual amount of hostility directed against his writings.

Comfort, whom Kenneth Rexroth has praised as having "a universality about him in many ways reminiscent of Albert Schweitzer,"[3] expresses a reverence for life in his works that is reminiscent of that of Schweitzer. His literary works, as well as his sociological and scientific writings, treat what he believes to be threats to life and human happiness and are characterized by compassion and a sense of identification with suffering humanity. Like other neo-Romantics he is to be understood as reacting against the influence of Eliot and Pound (emotional intensity, not concentration or intellectual complexity, is the essence of Romantic poetry). But partly because of his scientific orientation and scholarly background, his works often manifest a kind of virile rationality and Hellenic lucidity distinguishable from the generally more private, subjective works of neo-Romantics such as Thomas and Barker. If his writings were somewhat overrated during the war, they were underrated after the end of hostilities as reactions developed against radical thought and in literary circles against the excesses of neo-Romanticism. Like those of Barker and Henry Treece, his literary works are generally of interest and value artistically as well as of significance as indications of the character and diversity of neo-Romantic art.

Notes and References

Chapter One

1. "Alex Comfort," in *The Freedom of Poetry* (London, 1947), pp. 74–75.
2. In *The Penguin Companion to English Literature*, ed. David Daiches (New York, 1971), p. 114.
3. Thomas H. Helmstadter, *The Apocalyptic Movement in British Poetry* (unpub. doctoral dissertation, Univ. of Penn., 1963), p. xxix.
4. "Anarchism in Print: Yesterday and Today," in *Anarchism Today*, ed. David Apter and James Joll (New York, 1972), p. 154.
5. 7 August 1974 conversation with Comfort. Unless otherwise specified, the quotations appearing in part I of chapter one are from this source.
6. Hugh Kenner, "The Comfort behind *The Joy of Sex*," *New York Times Magazine*, Oct. 27, 1974, p. 81.
7. *Ibid.*, p. 72.
8. *Ibid.*
9. 7 August 1974 conversation.
10. "Alex Comfort's Art and Scope," *Anarchy*, 33 (November 1963), p. 345.
11. *Alexander Comfort and British New Romanticism. A Study of: The Silver River (1938), No Such Liberty (1941), The Almond Tree (1942), and The Power House (1944).* (Unpub. dissertation, Univ. of Washington, 1971), pp. 65–66.
12. 7 August 1974 conversation.
13. Callahan, pp. 104–105.
14. "English Poetry and the War," *Partisan Review* (March-April 1943), p. 192.
15. 7 August 1974 conversation.
16. *Ibid.*
17. Kenner, p. 19.
18. 7 August 1974 conversation.
19. Kenner, p. 74.
20. London, p. 2.
21. New York, 1956, trans. Anthony Bower, p. 247.
22. New York, 1956, trans. Justin O'Brien, p. 136.
23. *Art and Social Responsibility* (London, 1946), p. 15.
24. 3 August 1970, p. 52.

25. The experiments of C. M. McCay in the mid-1930s on underfeeding as a means of increasing the useful life-span of rats established definitely, and for the first time, that the life-span is subject to radical modification. The more recent use of chemical additives to increase the life-span of mice 30–45 percent appears to offer a more promising method of increasing the human life-span, but is a subject of some controversy. Comfort discusses McCay's work in *The Process of Ageing* (see pp. 53–56) and *Ageing: The Biology of Senescence* (p. 199 ff.).

26. 7 August 1974 conversation.

27. London, 1926, p. 9.

28. *Ibid.*

29. *Ibid.*, p. 106.

30. London, 1946, p. 17.

31. New York, 1963, p. 47.

32. "Anarchists in Britain Today," in *Anarchism Today*, ed. David Apter and James Joll (New York, 1972), p. 108.

33. pp. 113–14.

34. *Ibid.*, p. 113.

35. 7 August 1974 conversation.

36. *Ibid.*

37. *Ibid.*

38. *Ibid.*

39. *Ibid.*

40. *The Human Zoo* (New York, 1969), pp. 23–25.

41. 7 August 1974 conversation.

42. *The Human Zoo*, pp. 26–27.

43. *Ibid.*, p. 31.

44. 7 August 1974 conversation.

45. *Ibid.*

46. *Mutual Aid* (Boston, no pub. date), pp. 54–55.

47. "Notes on the Biology of Religion" is a paper presented to The Institute for Higher Studies by Comfort. Page numbers are not included since quotations appearing here are from a typewritten manuscript, a photocopy of which Dr. Comfort graciously sent to me, rather than from the final and complete version.

48. 7 August 1974 conversation.

49. "Notes on the Biology of Religion."

50. 7 August 1974 conversation.

51. "Notes on the Biology of Religion."

52. *Ibid.*

53. Boston, 1955, p. 207.

54. In *The Future of Sexual Relations*, ed. Robert T. and Anna K. Francoeur (Englewood Cliffs, New Jersey, 1974), p. 57.

55. New York, 1932, p. 31.

56. *Ibid.*, p. 313.
57. *Scientific American* (September 1960), p. 80.
58. In *Comparative Psychology Monogram*, 16, no. 5 (1940), p. 132.
59. *Ibid.*, p. 127.
60. p. 80.
61. *Ibid.*
62. "On Sexuality, Play and Earnest," *Le Domaine Humain*, VI, no. 1 (Spring 1974), p. 183.
63. New York, 1949, p. 20.

Chapter Two

1. p. 178.
2. p. 351.
3. p. 111.
4. London, 1951, p. 16.
5. "Alex Comfort as Novelist," *Limbo* (November 1964), p. 36.
6. "The Comedy of Ideas: Cross-currents in the Fiction and Drama of the Twentieth Century," *The Modern Age* (Vol. VII of the *Pelican Guide to English Literature*), ed. Boris Ford (Baltimore, 1963), pp. 225–26.
7. New York, 1968, pp. 307–309.
8. New York, 1928, p. 294.
9. p. 226.
10. Included in *The Collected Essays, Journalism and Letters of George Orwell*, eds. Sonia Orwell and Ian Angus, II (New York, 1968), pp. 166–67.
11. *Ibid.*, pp. 170–71. Orwell's criticism of the political implications of *No Such Liberty* foreshadows a controversy which developed the following year between Orwell and the writers of the New Romanticism: see "Pacifism and the War: A Controversy. By D. S. Savage, George Woodcock, Alex Comfort, George Orwell," *Partisan Review*, September-October 1942, pp. 414–21. The *Partisan Review* controversy, in turn, initiated an exchange of satiric poems (after the manner of Neoclassical occasional satires, packed with topical allusions) between Comfort and Orwell. In *Letter to an American Visitor* by Obadiah Hornbooke (*Tribune*, 4 June 1943), Comfort writes,

> You've seen the ruins, heard the speeches, swallowed
>   The bombed-out hospitals and cripples' schools—
> You've heard (on records) how the workers hollowed
>   And read in poker-work GIVE US THE TOOLS:
>   You know how, with the steadfastness of mules,
> The Stern Determination of the People
>   Goes sailing through a paradise of fools
> Like masons shinning up an endless steeple—
>   A climb concluding after many days
>   In a brass weathercock that points all ways. . . .

> Once in a while, to every Man and Nation,
>   There comes, as Lowell said, a sort of crisis
> Between the Ministry of Information
>   And what your poor artistic soul advises:
>   They catch the poets, straight from Cam or Isis:
> "Join the brigade, or be for ever dumb—
>   Either cash in your artistic lysis
> Or go on land work if you won't succumb:
>   Rot in the Army, sickened and unwilling":
>   So you can wonder that they draw their shilling? . . .
>
> O for another Dunciad—a POPE
>   To purge this dump with his gigantic boot—
> Drive fools to water, aspirin or rope—
>   Make idle lamp-posts bear their fitting fruit:
>   Private invective's far too long been mute—
> O for another vast satiric comet
>   To blast this wretched tinder, branch and root. . . .

Orwell's answer, *As One Non-Combatant to Another* (A Letter to "Obadiah Hornbooke"), published in the *Tribune*, 18 June 1943, is in part a poetic rendition of his arguments appearing in his review of *No Such Liberty* and in the *Partisan Review*. Orwell had argued in the *Partisan Review*,

What I object to is the intellectual cowardice of people who are objectively and to some extent emotionally pro-Fascist, but who don't care to say so and take refuge behind the formula "I am just as anti-Fascist as anyone, but—." . . .
It is tacitly pretended [by such pacifists] that the war is only between Britain and Germany. Mention of Russia and China, and their fate if Fascism is permitted to win, is avoided. (You won't find one word about Russia or China in the three letters you [i.e., Savage, Woodcock, and Comfort] sent me.) . . .
I have used a lot of ink and done myself a lot of harm by attacking the successive literary cliques which have infested this country, not because they were intellectuals but precisely because they were *not* what I mean by true intellectuals. The life of a clique is about five years and I have been writing long enough to see three of them come and go—the Catholic gang, the Stalinist gang, and the present Pacifist or, as they are sometimes nicknamed, Fascifist gang.

In *As One Non-Combatant to Another*, Orwell informs Comfort:

> O poet strutting from the sandbagged portal
>   Of that small world where barkers ply their art,
> And each new 'school' believes itself immortal,
>   Just like the horse that draws the knacker's cart:
> O captain of a clique of self-advancers,
>   Trained in the tactics of the pamphleteer. . . .
>
> You're a true poet, but as saint and martyr
> You're a mere fraud, like the Atlantic Charter. . . .

Your hands are clean, and so were Pontius Pilate's. . . .
To chalk a pavement doesn't need much guts,
It pays to stay at home and be a writer
While other talents wilt in Nissen huts. . . .

For while you write the warships ring you round
And flights of bombers drown the nightingales,
And every bomb that drops is worth a pound
To you or someone like you, for your sales
Are swollen with those of rivals dead or silent,
Whether in Tunis or the BBC,
And in the drowsy freedom of this island
You're free to shout that England isn't free;
They even chuck you cash, as bears get buns,
For crying "Peace!" behind a screen of guns. . . .

Your game is easy, and its rules are plain:
Pretend the war began in 'thirty-nine,
Don't mention China, Ethiopia, Spain, . . .

If you'd your way we'd leave the Russians to it
And sell our steel to Hitler as before;
Meanwhile you save your soul, and while you do it,
Take out a long-term mortgage on the war.
For after war there comes an ebb of passion,
The dead are sniggered at—and there you'll shine,
You'll be the very bull's-eye of the fashion,
You almost might get back to 'thirty-nine,
Back to the dear old game of scratch-my-neighbour
In sleek reviews financed by coolie labour.

The following month the tone of the controversy became less vitriolic. In a letter (11? July 1943), Orwell responded graciously to Comfort's gift of a copy of *New Road: New Directions in European Art and Letters:*

Dear Comfort,
Very many thanks for sending me the copy of *New Road*. I am afraid I was rather rude to you in our *Tribune* set-to, but you yourself weren't altogether polite to certain people. I was only making a *political* and perhaps moral reply, and as a piece of verse your contribution was immensely better, a thing most of the people who spoke to me about it hadn't noticed. I think no one noticed that your stanzas had the same rhyme going right the way through. There is no respect for virtuosity nowadays. You ought to write something longer in that genre, something like the "Vision of Judgement." I believe there could be a public for that kind of thing again nowadays.
    As to *New Road*. I am much impressed by the quantity and the general level of the verse you have got together. . . .

The verse epistles of Comfort and Orwell are reprinted in *The Oxford Book of*

Twentieth Century English Verse, ed. Philip Larkin (Oxford, 1973), pp. 513–21, and in Orwell's *Collected Essays,* II, 294–303.

12. *Ibid.*, p. 166.

13. pp. 123, 189, 135, 166, 177.

14. pp. 145, 177, 174.

15. p. 171.

16. p. 142.

17. Included in *The Essential Works of Anarchism,* ed. Marshall Shatz (New York, 1971), p. 252.

18. "Exposition of Irresponsibility" (October 1943), pp. 55–56.

19. Included in *Literary Criticism: Pope to Croce,* ed. Gay Allen and Harry Hayden Clark (Detroit, 1962), p. 595.

20. *The Freedom of Poetry,* pp. 101–102.

21. *Ibid.*, p. 101.

22. *Listener,* 13 August 1942, p. 218. Unless otherwise specified, the entire text of a review cited will be found on the page or pages designated.

23. *The Freedom of Poetry,* p. 98.

24. p. 218.

25. p. 207.

26. p. 106.

27. p. 197.

28. p. 102.

29. p. 353.

30. 14 October 1944, pp. 256–57.

31. 25 March 1945, p. 4.

32. 1 April 1945, p. 9.

33. 17 March 1945, pp. 11, 30.

34. 2 April 1945, pp. 450–51.

35. 31 March 1945, p. 368.

36. 29 September 1944, p. 296.

37. p. 34.

38. p. 322.

39. p. 35.

40. *Enquiry Concerning Political Justice* (Oxford University Press, 1971), p. 313.

41. In Thoreau's essay on civil disobedience, included in *The Anarchists,* ed. Irving Horowitz (New York, 1964), pp. 213, 215.

42. *The Parliament of Women: A Drama in Three Acts* (London, 1960), p. 37.

43. pp. 19–20.

44. p. 267.

45. Ed. Stefan Schimanski and Henry Treece (London, 1943), pp. 168, 165.

46. *Ibid.*, pp. 171–75.

47. *Art and Social Responsibility*, p. 19 (fn.). In 1974 Comfort spoke more simply of the awareness of mortality as involving "a general distaste for the cessation of experience" (7 August 1974 conversation).

Chapter Three

1. *The Cult of Power* (New York, 1947), p. 16.
2. New York, 1962, p. 147.
3. 9 January 1949, p. 6.
4. 9 January 1949, p. 16.
5. Summer 1949, pp. 315–16.
6. *Kenyon Review* (Spring 1950), p. 358. Review includes pp. 357–60.
7. *Arizona Quarterly* (Summer 1952), p. 101.
8. *Interim*, IV (1954), 87–88.
9. Trans. Bernard Frechtman (New York, 1964), p. 9.
10. Heningford Grey, England: Privately printed at the Vine Press, 1960, p. 37.
11. pp. 170–71.
12. p. 76.
13. "Alex Comfort as Novelist," p. 34.
14. Both novels treat "sham" anarchists, but reflect turn-of-the-century ideas about anarchists.
15. p. 349.
16. p. 360.
17. pp. 109, 111.
18. See, in particular, the excellent analysis of Kafka's personality in Vernon Grant's *This Is Mental Illness* (Boston, 1963), pp. 75–81.
19. 4 February 1949, p. 166.
20. Trans. Stuart Gilbert (New York, 1960), p. 116.
21. "Letter to Roland Barthes on *The Plague*," in *Lyrical and Critical Essays*, trans. Ellen Kennedy (New York, 1968), p. 340.
22. *The Rhetoric of Fiction* (Chicago, 1961), p. 297 (f.n.).
23. In *Selected Writings on Anarchism and Revolution*, ed. Martin Miller (Cambridge, Massachusetts, 1970), p. 338.
24. "Alex Comfort's Art and Scope," p. 351.
25. The novel contains a prefatory summary of its narrative structure.
26. Hugh Kenner, "The Comfort behind *The Joy of Sex*," p. 18.
27. 7 August 1974 conversation.
28. *Ibid.*
29. *Ibid.*
30. *Ibid.*
31. p. 57.
32. February 25, 1971, p. 412.
33. New York, 1972, p. 288.
34. 7 August 1974 conversation.

35. *Ibid.*
36. *Ibid.*
37. *Ibid.*

Chapter Four

1. *The Freedom of Poetry*, pp. 77–78.
2. October 1941, pp. 36–40.
3. "Apocalypse in poetry," in *The White Horseman*, ed. J. F. Hendry and Henry Treece (London, 1941), p. 10.
4. "Modern Poets and Reviewers," *Horizon* (June 1942), p. 436.
5. Henry Treece, *How I See Apocalypse* (London, 1946), p. 178
6. "Anarchism: What It Really Stands For," in *Anarchism*, ed. Robert Hoffman (New York, 1970), pp. 41–42.
7. *The Freedom of Poetry*, p. 81.
8. Moses I. Finley, *A History of Sicily: Ancient Sicily to the Arab Conquest* (London, 1968), I, p. 72.
9. *The Freedom of Poetry*, p. 83.
10. *The Tragic Sense of Life in Men and in Peoples*, trans. J. E. Flitch (London, 1931), p. 29.
11. *The Freedom of Poetry*, p. 85.
12. *Ibid.*, p. 86.
13. *Ibid.*, pp. 86–87.
14. *Ibid.*, p. 88.
15. "Anarchist Morality," in *Kropotkin's Revolutionary Pamphlets*, ed. Roger Baldwin (New York, 1927), p. 105.
16. *The Freedom of Poetry*, p. 90.
17. 3 March 1945, p. 141.
18. 24 August 1946, p. 2.
19. An allusion to Ovid's *Ars Amatoria*, III, 775 ff., according to a note to me from Comfort.
20. *Deipnosophistae*, XIII, 11. 588 ff.
21. According to a note to me from Comfort, the "reference is to the hail of leaves when a tree comes under crossfire."
22. "Alex Comfort's Art and Scope," p. 356.
23. *Encounter*, September 1962, p. 81.
24. *New Statesman*, 4 May 1962, p. 639.
25. According to a note to me from Comfort, Mister Pontius Paradise refers to Anthony Eden.
26. Before talking with Comfort I had assumed that the poem contained, as well, a probable reference to the political apostasy of Herbert Read in accepting knighthood. According to Comfort this is not the case, although he did say he had learned ("through the grapevine") that Read had taken personally Comfort's reference to "another" that "turned Knight."

Chapter Five

1. *Sense and Non-Sense*, trans. Hubert Dreyfus and Patricia Dreyfus (Northwestern University Press, 1964), p. 54.

2. 7 August 1974 conversation.

3. *The New British Poets: an Anthology*, ed. Kenneth Rexroth (Norfolk, Conn., 1949), p. xxviii.

Selected Bibliography

PRIMARY SOURCES

Ageing: The Biology of Senescence. London: Routledge & Kegan Paul, Ltd., 1964.

And All But He Departed. London: Routledge & Kegan Paul, Ltd., 1951.

The Almond Tree. London: Chapman & Hall, 1942.

The Anxiety Makers. London: Thomas Nelson & Sons, Ltd., 1967.

Art and Social Responsibility. London: Falcon Press, 1946.

Authority and Delinquency in the Modern State. London: Routledge & Kegan Paul, Ltd., 1950. Rev. 1970.

Barbarism and Sexual Freedom. London: Freedom Press, 1948.

The Besieged, Act One. *Life and Letters Today,* April 1944, pp. 32–48.

Cities of the Plain. London: Grey Walls Press, 1943.

Come Out to Play. London: Eyre & Spottiswoode, Ltd., 1961; New York: Crown Publishers, Inc., 1975.

"Communication May Be Odorous." *New Scientist and Science Journal,* 25 February 1971, pp. 412–14.

Darwin and the Naked Lady. New York: George Braziller, 1962.

Elegies. London: George Routledge & Sons, Ltd., 1944.

"English Poetry and the War." *Partisan Review,* March-April 1943, pp. 191–95.

"Exposition of Irresponsibility." *Life and Letters Today,* October 1943, pp. 52–58.

France and Other Poems. London: Favil Press, 1941.

"Freedon Press." *New Statesman and Nation,* 19 May 1945, p. 322.

"The Freedom Press Raid." *New Statesman and Nation,* 3 March 1945, p. 141. Co-signed by T. S. Eliot, E. M. Forster, Ethel Mannin, John Middleton Murry, Herbert Read, Reginald Reynolds, D. S. Savage, Stephen Spender, and Julian Symons.

A Giant's Strength. London: Routledge & Kegan Paul, Ltd., 1952.

Haste to the Wedding. London: Eyre & Spottiswoode, Ltd., 1962.

Into Egypt: A Miracle Play. Billericay: Grey Walls Press, 1942.

"It Goes Like This." *Life and Letters Today.* October 1941, pp. 36–40.

The Joy of Sex. New York: Crown Publishers, Inc., 1972.

The Koka Shastra. Trans. and with an Introd. by Alex Comfort. New York: Ballantine Books, 1965.

159

Letters from an Outpost. London: George Routledge & Sons, Ltd., 1947.
Lyra: an Anthology of New Lyric. Eds. Alex Comfort and Robert Greacen. Billericay: Grey Walls Press, 1942.
More Joy. New York: Crown Publishers, Inc., 1974.
Nature and Human Nature. London: Weidenfeld and Nicolson, 1966; Harmondsworth: Penguin Books, Ltd., 1969.
" 'Never Mind, Mr. Lom.' Alfred Lomnitz." Reviewed by Alex Comfort. *Life and Letters Today.* December 1941, pp. 226–28.
New Road 1944. Eds. Alex Comfort and John Bayliss. Billericay: Grey Walls Press, 1944.
No Such Liberty. London: Chapman & Hall, 1941.
The Novel and Our Time. London: Phoenix House, 1948.
"On Sexuality, Play and Earnest." *Le Domaine Humain,* VI. No. 1 (Spring 1974), 177–84.
On This Side Nothing. London: Routledge & Kegan Paul, Ltd., 1949; New York: Viking Press, 1949.
"Pacifism and the War: A Controversy." *Partisan Review.* September-October 1942, pp. 414–21. With D. S. Savage, George Woodcock, and George Orwell.
The Pattern of the Future. London: Routledge & Kegan Paul, Ltd., 1950.
Poetry Folios. Eds. Alex Comfort and Peter Wells. Barnett: The Editors, 1942–46.
The Power House. London: George Routledge & Kegan Paul, Ltd., 1944; New York: Viking, 1945.
Sex in Society. London: Gerald Duckworth & Co., Ltd., 1963; Secaucus, New Jersey: The Citadel Press, 1975.
Sexual Behavior in Society. London: Gerald Duckworth & Co., Ltd., 1950.
"Sexuality in a Zero Growth Society." *The Future of Sexual Relations.* Eds. Robert T. and Anna K. Francoeur. Englewood Cliffs: Prentice-Hall, Inc., 1974, pp. 52–57.
The Process of Ageing. New York: New American Library, 1961.
The Signal to Engage. London: George Routledge & Sons, Ltd., 1947.
The Silver River: Being the Diary of a Schoolboy in the South Atlantic, 1936. London: Chapman & Hall, 1938.
"Social Causes of Ill Health." *Freedom.* 24 August 1946, p. 2. (A review of John Hewetson's *Ill-Health, Poverty and the State.*)
The Song of Lazarus. New York: Viking, 1945.
The Triumph of Death. Trans. Alex Comfort and Ross MacDougall. London: George Routledge & Sons, Ltd., 1946.
A Wreath for the Living. London: George Routledge & Sons, Ltd., 1942.

SECONDARY SOURCES

BURNS, WAYNE. "Kafka and Alex Comfort: The Penal Colony Revisited." *Arizona Quarterly* (Summer 1952), 101–20. Perceptive psychoanalytical comparison of Kafka's *The Penal Colony* and Comfort's *On This Side Nothing*.

————. "Milton and Alex Comfort." *Interim,* 4 (1954), 87–89. Contains Comfort's explanation of his reason for selecting the title of *On This Side Nothing* (as recorded in a letter to Burns) and Burns's conjectures on the title's meaning to the novel.

————. "The Scientific Humanism of Alex Comfort." *The Humanist,* 11 (November 1951), 269–274. Sensible interpretation of *The Pattern of the Future,* a book containing the text of four of Comfort's BBC broadcasts of 1949.

CALLAHAN, ROBERT. *Alexander Comfort and British New Romanticism. A Study of: The Silver River (1939), No Such Liberty (1941), The Almond Tree (1942), and The Power House (1944).* Unpub. dissertation, Univ. of Washington, 1971. Provides an extensive and generally competent analysis of Comfort's first three novels and *The Silver River.*

————. "A Bibliography in Progress." *West Coast Review* (Winter 1969), 48–67. Callahan's bibliography, which "with certain qualifications," attempts to "cite all writing by or about Alexander Comfort, published as of December 31, 1967," will prove to be a significant contribution to advanced studies of Comfort's works. It is based on Drasdo's bibliography (see below) and titles provided by Comfort from his "personal scrapbooks."

DOHENY, JOHN. "Alex Comfort as Novelist." *Limbo* (November 1964), 29–43. Covers the last four novels: *The Power House, On This Side Nothing, A Giant's Strength,* and *Come Out to Play.* Doheny's criticism is often shrewd and based in part on personal knowledge and appreciation of Comfort: in a letter to me he writes that he has known Comfort "since the early 1950s" and has "always argued that his work is some of the most significant in this century."

DRASDO, HAROLD. "Alex Comfort's Art and Scope." *Anarchy,* 33 (November 1963), 45–58. Treats Comfort's *The Silver River,* his novels, short stories, poetry, and literary criticism, and provides a bibliography of Comfort's works. Drasdo attempts to do too much in an article of very limited length, but his critical survey, touching upon a number of Comfort's works published after Stanford's study (see below), and his bibliography will be of particular interest to readers who are beginning their study of Comfort's works.

STANFORD, DEREK. "Alex Comfort," *The Freedom of Poetry.* London: Falcon Press, 1947. The first general study of Comfort's literary works. It relates his works to a contemporary literary background and is generally a preceptive and helpful introduction to Comfort's art.

Index

163